Risk Assessment of Food Supply

Risk Assessment of Food Supply: A Computable General Equilibrium Approach

By

Tetsuji Tanaka
with Nobuhiro Hosoe and Huanguang Qiu

CAMBRIDGE SCHOLARS
PUBLISHING

Risk Assessment of Food Supply:
A Computable General Equilibrium Approach,
by Tetsuji Tanaka with Nobuhiro Hosoe and Huanguang Qiu

This book first published 2012

Cambridge Scholars Publishing

12 Back Chapman Street, Newcastle upon Tyne, NE6 2XX, UK

British Library Cataloguing in Publication Data
A catalogue record for this book is available from the British Library

ISBN (10): 1-4438-4183-8, ISBN (13): 978-1-4438-4183-2

To my parents

Contents

ACKNOWLEDGEMENTS

This book is based on my PhD thesis at the School of Oriental and African Studies, University of London. I would like to express my deep and respectful gratitude to my PhD programme supervisor, Professor Laixiang Sun. Over the course of the past three years, he has given me truly valuable and practical advice not only on research, but also for my career path. In addition, I would like to thank Professor Noriyuki Goto, Dr Hiroyuki Kawashima, and Professor Masayoshi Honma at University of Tokyo for their very valuable comments on my research work. My gratitude also goes to my friends, fellow researchers and staff at School of Oriental and African Studies for their generous supports and encouragement during my PhD study. I want to thank the examiners of my thesis, Professor Andrew Dorward and Dr Lionel Hubbard, for their patience for careful reading of the thesis and thoughtful and constructive comments.

My parents Mr Toshihiko and Mrs Fukiko Tanaka and my brother Shugo Tanaka deserve a great amount of gratitude for their generosity and assistance. My parents firmly supported my long student life financially and emotionally. When I faced tough times, they always offered me warm words and crucial encouragement.

I am also grateful to the Cambridge Scholars Publishing for granting me an opportunity to publish the book. I regret any errors that may appear in this book and take full responsibility for them.

DR TETSUJI TANAKA

LIST OF TABLES AND FIGURES

Tables

Figures

CHAPTER ONE

INTRODUCTION

TETSUJI TANAKA

Motivation and objective

While it is acknowledged that the occurrence of a food crisis follows roughly a 30-year cycle (Naylor and Falcon, 2010), food prices rose sharply twice in 2008 and 2010. The recent food price rise has pushed 44 million more people into poverty since June 2010 and the food price turbulence in 2008 drove 100 million people into poverty (World Bank, 2011). These two very recent crises may suggest that access to food is becoming more difficult now and in the near future. In addition to the traditional factors of population and income growth in BRICs (Brazil, Russia, India, and China), which would lead to a slow increase in food demand, the striking food price turbulence in recent years may be more closely associated with the following new factors: biofuel production, financial globalisation, expansion of food speculation and climate change, among others.

Biofuel production has grown rapidly over the last ten years. The US and Brazil are large producers of bioethanol, which are produced mainly from maize and sugarcane, respectively. In 2008, over 30% of maize production in the US - the largest producer of maize - went to ethanol factories.[1] The EU is the largest producing region of biodiesel, which is mostly manufactured from soybean and oilseeds. Huge amounts of all grain produced in the world are now used for industrial purposes.

Many multilateral and bilateral free trade agreements have been concluded for agricultural products. While trade liberalisation is said to enhance the efficiency of resource allocation, nations deepen their interdependency on food through these agreements and become more susceptible to shocks from abroad such as poor harvests and embargoes.

[1] The share of maize used as feedstock in the US is estimated by the author.

Speculation has increased in food markets and was widely criticised as the root cause for the grain price bubble in 2008. Nicolas Sarkozy, the president of France, insisted at the 2011 G20 meeting that "France wants great transparency and regulation of commodities prices and derivative trading to stop being driven by speculation" (Rowley, 2011). Not only the G20 but the Food and Agriculture Organisation (FAO) also points out that speculation is the largest fundamental factor of the recent food crisis (Aloisi, 2011).

Some developing economies such as China and India, the first and second most populous countries in the world, are growing markedly. There is a historical trend that income growth increases meat consumption in terms of total calorie intake. In reality, meat consumption per capita in China grows as its economy develops, according to the FAOSTAT, which suggests that more grain is demanded for livestock feed.

Global food production can be damaged where climate change brings extreme weather pattern. Severe droughts devastated Australia's crop harvest in 2006 and 2007. Russia and Ukraine's grain production declined by as much as 38%, and they imposed a ban on their grain exports in 2010, which may have raised the world's wheat price by 58% according to Madon (2010). In recent years, more floods, droughts, and typhoons seem to have affected agricultural production.

One of the most important new factors is trade liberalisation over agricultural products as agricultural sectors are frequently contentious elements in negotiations of food security. Apart from industrial countries which maintain high food self-sufficiency rate like the U.S or Australia, industrialisation tends to undermine agricultural sectors' comparative advantage. Even the self-sufficiency rate of those European countries which are considered to be large agricultural regions has been declining since the late 1990s, and Asian countries like Japan, Taiwan and Korea show even clearer declining trends with their economic development. With many developed nations facing difficulty in feeding themselves, it is becoming ever more important to think about agricultural free trade issues from the viewpoint of food security for advanced and emerging nations such as China.

The most archetypal country is Japan. It achieved dramatic economic growth after the Second World War, and its food self-sufficiency rate on a calorie basis was about 80% in 1960, but only 40% after 1998. However, Japan is almost self-sufficient in rice, the primary diet, although the country currently imports 8% for the minimum access opportunities of the World Trade Organisation (WTO). This is a result of the strict protection by a high tariff of around 800%. Japan has long been called on to abolish the high tariff on rice by other countries, but has refused for its food security concern.

As stated, food interdependency between countries can facilitate the international transmission of food prices by lowering trade barriers. The world food market volatility in 2008 immediately spilt over to the economies of various regions, and some countries implemented grain export restrictions to curb domestic prices, which made the international market tighter and drove food prices several times higher. As a consequence, riots occurred in many areas of the world. In 2009, after the food crisis, a G8 summit was held to find international consensus on food price stabilisation policy. However, the effectiveness of these policies is in doubt because the fundamental causes behind the food price spikes were not yet fully clarified. Hence, it is essential to evaluate the impacts of potential risk factors on the world market's food prices.

A major question which agricultural and development economists have long struggled to answer is whether or not high agricultural prices are beneficial for developing economies (Aksoy and Izik-Dikmelik, 2008; Ivanic and Martin, 2008; Barrett and Dorosh, 1996; Ravallion and Lokshin, 2005). There are many publications on this subject, but the fundamental causes of grain price rises in poor countries have not been sufficiently examined. This is despite the fact that the rampages of the 2008 food crisis happened only in destitute regions, which implies that people in the developing world suffered more severely than those in rich economies.

As has been noted, developed and developing countries have individual factors for food security. This book evaluates the impacts of potential risk factors on food prices, and identifies policy implications for stabilising the food market. It does this through three empirical studies: one focusing on assessing the effects of rice trade liberalisation in Japan; a second identifying the underlying factors of the 2008 food price spikes, and a third establishing the contributory factors behind grain price rises in the least developed countries (LDCs).

Methodological issues

Computable general equilibrium (CGE) models are employed in the book. These are based on the general equilibrium framework developed by L. Walras and rooted in the work of Johansen (1960) who is widely regarded to have established the first CGE model. They have mainly been used in the areas of international trade, agriculture, development and environment.

CGE is suitable for agricultural research as agricultural sectors have become more deeply related to other sectors such as energy in recent years. Biofuel production from food materials such as maize, sugarcane, and oilseeds grew rapidly in the last decade. It can also influence the oil price as a substitute, and this affects agricultural production for intermediate input. Given this context, models that can capture the interactive effects between the industries are needed to analyse agricultural and/or food sectors. Hence, CGE can be a powerful tool in these research fields.

Another reason is the convenience of building a world-scale model. All three research topics in the book are relevant to international trade, which means that a global trade model is indispensable. Generally, collecting data to develop international models takes considerable costs, but for over a decade the Global Trade Analysis Project (GTAP) has contributed to a dataset called a social accounting matrix (SAM) for world models (Hertel, 1997). The GTAP's latest version of the global SAM has 113 regions of the world and 57 sectors. Today, the international interactive effects cannot be overlooked, taking into account the unification of European countries and lower trade barriers between countries. For this reason, it is appropriate to apply CGE models to the agricultural policy issues addressed in the book.

On the other hand, an often noted major weakness of CGE models is the unreliability of parameter estimation. In the process of building CGE models called "calibration", various parameters are estimated from the SAM used in the study.[2] A SAM is composed of a single-year data, which suggests that the parameters heavily depend on the year of a SAM. Conversely, this is an advantage of CGE models, and is a reason for which CGE is often used in development research in which data is often difficult to be collected. Yet, Valenzuela and Hertel (2007), for example, have demonstrated the validity of CGE models in the field of agriculture with some other publications also examining the reliability of the performances of CGE models in energy and international trade (Beckman et al., 2011; and Hertel et al., 2007).

Note on the database

The primary data set for the book is the global SAM from the GTAP. The latest version 7.2 of the GTAP has 57 industrial sectors and 113 regions, which are aggregated according to the purpose of the research. Elasticity of substitution is essential in CGE analysis. Most elasticity values are cited from the GTAP database although some elasticities

[2] See Section 2.5 for calibration.

estimated econometrically by existing literature are applied to the model.

Biofuel sectors do not exist in the latest GTAP database. For the purpose of this research, we need to introduce bioethanol and biodiesel sectors into the original database by estimating the relevant values of the sectors partly following the technique of Taheripour (2007). This article uses software called "SplitCom" to make new sectors in the GTAP database, but we insert them into the original data on our General Algebraic Modelling System (GAMS) programme.[3]

The SAM used in the book is based on 2004. The base year of CGE analysis is required to be in a situation like "equilibrium". The IMF Commodity Prices indicate monthly time-series world agricultural prices in which food prices do not show large price volatilities over the year of 2004. Thus, it can be considered that the GTAP database version 7 meets the conditions for being the base year of our analyses.

Contributions of the research

This book makes a methodological contribution and identifies several policy implications. First, most studies on Japan's rice trade liberalisation examines deterministic effects by a partial and general equilibrium model. Yet, for the empirical study in Chapter 3 we develop a stochastic CGE model with the Monte Carlo method to make it possible to assess the probabilistic impacts of rice productivities, which enables us to answer how risky rice trade liberalisation is for Japan. The Monte Carlo estimation in CGE is unconventional, and can make a solid contribution to the area.

Some important policy implications are noted by the book. On the topic of the Japanese government's rice trade liberalisation policy, existing articles focus on deterministic gains/losses (Cramer et al., 1999; Cramer et al., 1993; Wailes, 2005) but fail to answer a serious concern in Japan that rice export embargoes may be carried out by export partners after relying more on imports. Our study overcomes the long-standing problem by developing a stochastic CGE model.

Many reports explore the possible factors behind the food crisis in 2008. However, most employ a descriptive method. Some articles estimate the impact of export restrictions, oil price hikes and biofuel production (Charlebois, 2008; Yang et al., 2008; Mitchell, 2008; and Rosegrant, 2008) but other factors such as crop failures by drought are not investigated. In addition, it is important to assess the effects of potential factors in one

---

[3] The GAMS is a programming language. This is more explained in Chapter 2.

model in order to compare the magnitude of influences. We identify the risk factors, measuring the effects of poor harvests in Australia and Ukraine, export restrictions by major exporters, the oil price spike and biofuel production.

Analyses of the relationship between high food prices and poverty in developing countries can be roughly classified into three groups. The first category considers whether high food prices increase poverty in developing countries (Aksoy and Izik-Dikmelik, 2008; Ivanic and Martin, 2008; Barrett and Dorosh, 1996; Ravallion and Lokshin, 2005). The second examines the price transmission from global to regional markets (Arndt et al, 2009 and Cudjoe et al., 2010). The final group clarifies factors threatening domestic markets in developing economies (Yang et al., 2008; Nganou et al., 2009; Parra and Wodon, 2008). These studies analyse the impacts of high oil price and biofuel on food price in a specific country like China and Kenya. However, the investigated regions are not extremely poor countries such as those least developed countries (LDCs) which suffered more severe damages from food inflation. Therefore, we will clarify how much the risk factors affected the 2008 price spikes in LDCs.

Organisation of the book

Chapter 2 describes the methodology used for the studies by explaining the structure of SAMs, CGE models and the Monte Carlo method. Chapter 3 analyses Japan's rice trade liberalisation policy. Chapters 4, 5 and 6 contain two types of analyses: the analysis of the factors underlying the food price increases in the world markets; and the identification of potential determinants of the grain price rises in LDCs. Chapter 4 gives the introduction and literature survey. Chapter 5 conducts a critical review of the models in the past literature, and explains our methodology. Chapter 6 shows the simulation results and discusses the policy implications. Finally, Chapter 7 concludes the whole book.

CHAPTER TWO

COMPUTABLE GENERAL EQUILIBRIUM MODEL

TETSUJI TANAKA

Introduction

The general equilibrium theory developed by L. Walras was refined by K. Arrow and G. Debreu to discuss the existence and the stability of competitive equilibrium. However, their models are abstract and so cannot be applied to real economic problems. As explained below, the general equilibrium theory has evolved to become a useful tool for policy analysis, used by many economists.

Figure 2.1 shows the basic idea of a CGE model. Households supply their factors of production such as labour and capital to the market while firms demand them for their production. Firms produce commodities and services, and households consume them. The demand and supply of production factors and commodities are adjusted on markets through the price mechanism. Households and firms maximise their utility and profit under the budget constraint and production technology, respectively.

CGE models originated from input-output (IO) models developed by Wassily W. Leontief, although price and quantity are not independently endogenous in IO models.[1] The prototype of CGE models is Johansen (1960) and Harberger (1962). Furthermore, Scarf (1967), who numerically solved the Arrow-Debreu general equilibrium, contributed to developing various applications of the models. Dervis et al. (1982) constructed CGE models for developing economies, whilst models for tax and international trade issues in advanced countries were built by Shoven and Whalley (1992). Although the models can be applied to a wide range of areas, most models have been made for international trade. The GTAP model and

---

[1] Exactly, applied general equilibrium (AGE) models are not identical to CGE models. Yet, for simplicity both are standardised to CGE in this book. See Mitra-Kahn (2008) for more explanations.

database, a global CGE model and SAM, have played a great role in the development of trade policy analysis (Hertel, 1997).

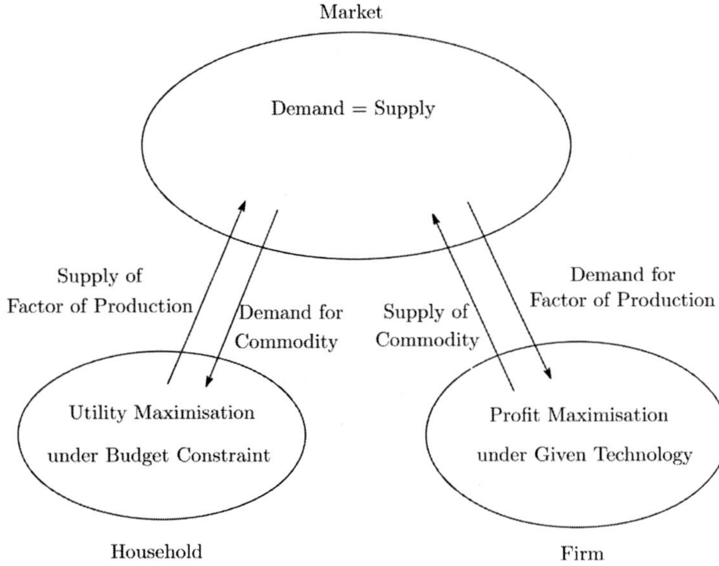

Figure 2.1: Concept of a CGE model

Whalley (1982) conducted one of the pioneering works analysing trade policies using the general equilibrium frame work in a numerical fashion. It evaluates the effects of the various formulae proposed in the Tokyo Round negotiations under the General Agreement on Tariffs and Trade (GATT). CGE models have since been more widely used to discuss multi-regional trade issues with the GTAP model and database as described. Initially, it was often applied to the North American Free Trade Agreement (NAFTA) and multilateral trade negotiations under the GATT/WTO. Many of the important articles on the NAFTA and the Uruguay Round analysed by CGE are introduced by Francois and Shiells (1994) and Martin and Winters (1996), respectively.

Studies scrutinising the international trade issues are categorised roughly into five groups: reduction/abolishment of trade barriers for industrial products; trade barriers/subsidy for agricultural products; trade barriers for service sectors; trade facilitation; and others such as foreign direct investment and the liberalisation of capital and labour mobility. The third and fourth categories, trade barriers for service and trade facilitation, are more difficult to analyse in terms of quantifying the trade barriers. The estimates of the barriers differ greatly between papers because the data and methods for the estimation used are not agreed. This is still an important subject in this area.

While the GTAP model is regarded as a standard model in international trade CGE analyses, the Michigan model by University of Michigan and the Francois model by Francois into which economies of scale and imperfect competition are introduced were built with the development of the new trade theory by Krugman (1980).[2] The Francois model has a similar structure to the GTAP model but discards the Armington assumption. In the Michigan model, the Cobb-Douglas utility function is employed, and the Armington assumption is not made. Also, recursive dynamic models such as the LINKAGE model by the World Bank and the MIRAGE model by the Centre d'Etudes Prospectives et d'Informations Internationals (CEPII) have since been constructed.[3] The LINKAGE model adopts the perfect competition assumption while the MIRAGE model assumes imperfect competition and economy of scale.

Given the specific topics of this book, rice trade liberalisation in Japan and the grain price rises in the world market and LDCs' economies, some major strengths and weaknesses of CGE analyses should be mentioned. First, a CGE model can capture the spillover effects of the paddy and processed rice trade liberalisation on other various sectors such as service sectors, which is important especially when evaluating household welfare changes related to a variety of consumption goods and services. Second, it can consider repercussion effects. Today, food security has a complex structure with agricultural production, biofuels, oil, fertiliser and transport, which are related to each other. The complicated structure is well expressed on an IO data matrix. Hence, CGE simulations have an advantage. On the other hand, a weakness is that if import share is zero in the base data, the import remains zero even after abolishing trade barriers, which means that if Japan did not import rice from country A in the base year, the country does not export it to Japan after liberalisation. This suggests the possibility of the overestimation of the negative impacts on household welfare. Another disadvantage is that CGE cannot explicitly consider financial markets. Therefore, although financial speculation and

---

[2] See Hertel (1997), http://www.fordschool.umich.edu/rsie/model/ and Francois and Roland-Holst (1997) for the information on the GTAP, Michigan and Francois models.

[3] See Mensbrugghe (2005) and Bchir et al. (2002) for the LINKAGE and MIRAGE models.

US dollar depreciation are considered to be important potential factors for the world's grain price spikes, their effects cannot be quantified directly by CGE models. To overcome this difficulty, financial CGE models have been developed, but they are not sufficiently applicable yet.

We will discuss rice trade liberalisation in Japan in Chapter 3. This is a long-debated issue, but still Japan's government imposes very high tariffs on rice imports to protect domestic rice farmers. Economists have struggled to demonstrate benefits or losses from liberalisation. However, one of the largest unanswered questions is whether or not Japan secures reliable food supply by liberalising the rice market. To assess the risk, we develop a stochastic CGE model using the Monte Carlo method, and answer the question in Chapter 3.

A CGE model is formulated as a nonlinear programming problem or nonlinear simultaneous equations. To solve this problem, we use the General Algebraic Modelling System (GAMS). The GAMS was developed by the World Bank to analyse developing economies (Hosoe et al., 2010). The main features are that it is possible to directly programme algebraic equations and it has powerful algorism to solve complex problems. Thus, GAMS has been a standard language for CGE modellers.

In this chapter, firstly the structure of a SAM will be explained using a simple and global SAM composed of the GTAP database. Next, we will introduce a standard static single-country CGE model. Then, the model is extended to a global scale. Finally, the modifications of the world model for the empirical studies of this book are delineated.

Social accounting matrix (SAM)

Simple social accounting matrix

A SAM describes commodity and monetary flows of an economy for a certain period (usually one year). It is based on the input-output table developed by Wassily W. Leontief, and is constructed by combining an IO table with some additional data such as household savings.[4] The total of each heading is equal, suggesting demand and supply (or revenue and expenditure) are balanced. Like an IO table, the columns and rows of a SAM represent buyers and sellers, which mean that commodities flow from the column to row headings, and monetary flows conversely go from the row to column headings.

---

[4] Regarding the way of construction, see Hosoe et al. (2010).

Table 2.1: Example of a social accounting matrix

Unit: £

		Production Activities		Production Factors		Indirect Tax		Final Consumption			Foreign Countries	Total
		Wheat	Rice	Capital Stock	Labour	Production Tax	Import Tariff	Household	Government	Investment		
Production Activities	Wheat	12	30					38	2	1	7	90
	Rice	13	17					60	4	10	8	112
Production Factors	Capital Stock	10	9									19
	Labour	45	42									87
Indirect Tax	Production Tax	2	4									6
	Import Tariff	3	2									5
Final Consumption	Household			19	87							106
	Government					6	5	5				16
	Investment							3	10		-2	11
Foreign Countries		5	8									13
Total		90	112	19	87	6	5	106	16	11	13	

Table 2.1 shows a simplified SAM. The table includes the following sections: production activities, production factors, indirect tax, final consumption, and foreign countries.

Final consumption

In Table 2.1, (Wheat, Household) signifies that households consume £38 worth of wheat, and that wheat producer receives £38 from households.[5] In the same way, (Rice, Household) indicates that households consume £60 worth of rice, and that rice producers are paid £60 by households. Similarly, (Wheat, Government) and (Wheat, Investment) displays that £2 and £1 worth of wheat are consumed by the government and the investment (investor), which pay the money to producers.

Production activities

In the table, (Production Activities, Production Activities) shows intermediate input. (Rice, Wheat) demonstrates that £13 worth of rice is input into wheat production, and that rice producers receive £13 for offering rice from wheat producers. Likewise, £30 and £17 worth of wheat and rice are used for rice production, and wheat and rice producers receive £30 and £17, respectively.

Factors of production

The factors of production in the table are labour and capital stock. (Capital Stock, Wheat) shows that £10 is paid to owners of capital such as tractors by wheat farmers for lending the tractors. (Labour, Rice) also designates that people who worked for rice production receive £42 from rice producers for offering labour force.

The cell (Final Consumption, Production Factors) suggests the income of each economic agent such as household, government, and investment. For instance, households supply £45 and £42 worth of labour force to wheat and rice production, respectively. The total amount of income is displayed in the cell (Household, Labour) and (Household, Capital), which are £87 and £19, respectively. The income of the government is tax revenue. The cells (Indirect Tax, Production Activities) go to the government. For instance, the production tax for wheat and rice are £2 and £4, respectively. The total production tax revenue is displayed in the cell of (Government, Production Tax), which is £6. The sources of revenue for investors are the savings of the household, government, and foreign countries. They are described in the cell of (Investment, Household),

[5] In this chapter, (x,y) is x=row and y=column.

(Investment, Government), and (Investment, Foreign Countries), which are £3, £10, and -£2, respectively.

Indirect tax

Indirect tax is imposed on productions. For example, (Wheat, Production Tax) shows that wheat producers pay £2 to the government. (Wheat, Import Tariff) indicates that £3 is paid to the government when importing wheat from other countries.

Foreign countries

The cell (Foreign Countries, Rice) shows rice imports from abroad: the country imports £8 worth of rice from other countries. The imported commodities are used for both intermediate inputs and final consumption. The cell (Rice, Foreign Countries) signifies rice export. It shows that £8 worth of rice is exported to foreign countries.

IO tables are usually updated once in several years by national governments. If one needs a particular year-base SAM, he can update it using the RAS method.[6] The next section will extend it to a world scale using the GTAP database.

Global social accounting matrix with the GTAP database

The previous section outlined a basic single-country SAM. An international SAM differs particularly in trade sectors, but the commodity/service and monetary flows can be read in the same way. This section describes the structure of a global SAM fed with the GTAP database.

Table 2.2 indicates the structure of an international SAM composed of the GTAP database. The unit of value is in millions of US dollars in the GTAP database. The necessary data provided by the GTAP database for a world SAM is shown in Table 2.3.[7] The dimensions are different from those of the single-country SAM shown in the previous section (Table 2.4). The additional data are export duties, factor use taxes, transport margins on imports, exports of transport services and trade balance. The export duties are generated with exports; these are often negative values in agricultural sectors and mean export subsidy. The factor use taxes are imposed on labour, capital, farm land, and natural resources. In the GTAP

[6] RAS stands for Richard A. Stone who established the approach to update IO tables. See Parikh (1979).

[7] See McDonald and Thiefelder (2004) for constructing a SAM with the GTAP database.

SAM Table 2.2: Structure of a global GTAP with the database

	Production Activities	Factors	Production Taxes	Import Tariff	Export Tax	Factor Taxes	Household	Government	Investment	International Transport	Foreign Countires
Production Activities	Intermediate Inputs +Supply Matrix						Private Demand	Government Demand	Investment Demand	Exports of Transport Services	Exports of Goods and Services
Factors	Payments to Factors										
Production Taxes	Production Taxes										
Import Tariff	Import Duties										
Export Tax	Export Duties										
Factor Taxes	Factor Use Taxes										
Household		$\Sigma Payments$									
Government			$\Sigma Production\ Taxes$	$\Sigma Import\ Duties$	$\Sigma Export\ Duties$	$\Sigma Factor\ Use\ Taxes$	Direct Tax				
Investment							H.hold Saving	Gov. Saving		Trade Balance	Foreign Saving
International Transport	Transport Margins on Imports										
Foreign Countires	Imports of Goods and Services										

database and model, the international transport sector is considered, which suggests that transportation fees are levied with the transaction of imports/exports. So, importers pay a fee for their imports to international transport service firms, and this appears in transport margins on imports. Contrarily, companies exporting global transport services receive a fee from importers, which is expressed on export of transport services.

Table 2.3: Data for constructing a global SAM provided from the GTAP database

Supply Side	Demand Side	Others
Supply Matrix	Intermediate Inputs	Household Saving
Payments to Factors	Private Demand	
Production Taxes	Government Demand	
Import Duties	Investment Demand	
Export Duties	Exports of Transport Services	
Factor Use Taxes	Exports of Goods and Services	
Transport Margins on Imports		
Imports of Goods and Demands		

Table 2.4: Dimensions of the elements in the GTAP database

Dimension (j,r)	Dimension (j,r,s)	Dimension (r)	Dimension (i,j,r)	Dimension (h,j,r)
Production Taxes	Import Duties	Household Saving	Supply Matrix	Payments to Factors
Private Demand	Export Duties		Intermediate Inputs	Factor Use Taxes
Government Demand	Exports of Transport Services			
Investment Demand	Exports of Goods and Services			
	Transport Margins on Imports			
	Imports of Goods and Demands			

Note: i, r, and h signify goods and services, regions, and factors, respectively. j and s are the alias for i and r.

To make a completed intermediate input matrix, an intermediate inputs matrix and a supply matrix are doubled. In the same way as the simple SAM, payments to factors are added to make the total income for households (Household, Factors). Taxes imposed on production, import, export, and factor use are also added to make the tax revenue of the government ((Government, Production Taxes), (Government, Import Tariff), (Government, Export Tax), and (Government, Factor Taxes)). Given household saving data, direct tax is estimated by:

$\sum$ Payments – (Private Demand + H.hold Saying)

Then, Trade balance and foreign saving are computed by (Transport Margins on Imports–Exports of Transport Services) and (Imports of Goods and Services –Exports of Goods and Services). Similarly, government saving is calculated by (Investment Demand – Foreign Saving – Trade Balance – H.hold Saving).

CGE model

A single country CGE model

In this section, we will give information on a standard static single-country CGE model.[8] Figure 2.2 is the model structure for one sector. We will explain from the bottom to the top.

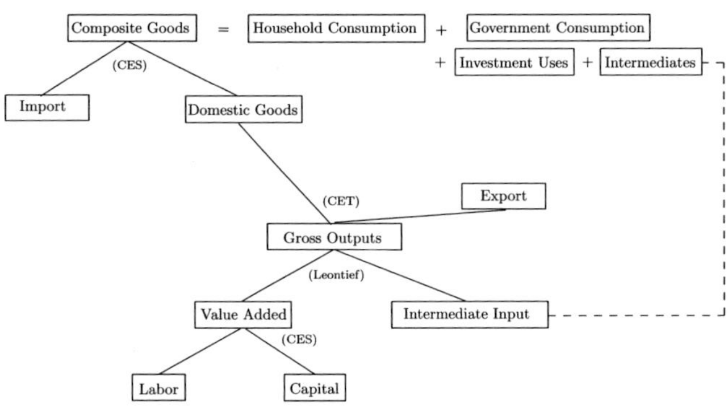

Figure 2.1: The structure of a single-country CGE model

Intermediate input (Equation (2.1.)-(2.6.))

Factors of production such as labour and capital are combined to produce a composite commodity of production factor (Equation (2.1.)). A firm varies the input ratio between labour and capital in response to the relative price so that the domestic representative firm maximises its profit. The function is a constant elasticity of substitution (CES) form here, but the Cobb-Douglas form is also often applied. The factor composite commodity is input with the intermediate inputs for domestic production (Equation (2.5.)). The production function is the Leontief form (Equation (2.3.)).

[8] See Hosoe et al. (2010) for the application of a SAM to a CGE model.

-Value added producing firm Factor demand function

$$F_{h,j} = \left(\frac{b_j^{\eta_j^{va}} \beta_{h,j} p_j^y}{p_{h,j}^f} \right)^{\frac{1}{1-\eta_j^{va}}} Y_j \qquad \forall j \quad (2.1.)$$

Value added production function

$$Y_j = b_j \left(\sum_h \beta_{h,j} F_{h,j}^{\eta_j^{va}} \right)^{1/\eta_j^{va}} \qquad \forall j \quad (2.2.)$$

-Gross output producing firm

Production function: $$Z_j = \min \left(\frac{X_{i,j}}{ax_{i,j}}, \frac{Y_j}{ay_j} \right) \qquad \forall j \quad (2.3.)$$

Demand function for intermediates

$$X_{i,j} = ax_{i,j} Z_j \qquad \forall i,j \quad (2.4.)$$

Demand function for value added

$$Y_j = ay_j Z_j \qquad \forall j \quad (2.5.)$$

Unit price function

$$p_{j,r}^z = ay_j p_j^y + \sum_i ax_{i,j} p_i^q \qquad \forall j \quad (2.6.)$$

Sets

i, j	: commodities/sectors
h	: factors (capital (CAP), land(LAN), labour(LAB))

Variables

Y_j	: value added
$F_{h,j}$	: factor uses
Z_j	: gross output
$X_{i,j}$	: intermediate uses of the i-th good by the j-th sector
p_j^y	: price of value added

$p^f_{h,j}$: price of factors

p^z_i : price of gross output

p^q_i : price of Armington composite goods

Parameters

b_j : scale parameter of production function for Yj

$\beta_{h,j}$: share parameter of factor input

σ^f_j : elasticity of substitution for a value added composite function

$ax_{i,j}$: share parameter of intermediate input for domestic production

ay_j : share parameter of composite factor input for domestic production

η^{va}_j : elasticity parameter $\eta^{va}_j = \frac{\sigma^f_j + 1}{\sigma^f_j}$

International trade (Equation (2.7.)-(2.15.))

Products produced by the representative firm are allocated to foreign countries (export) or to the domestic market. At this stage, we assume a firm converts the products according to the needs of the domestic market or the international market. It is also assumed that the company responds to the relative price changes between international and domestic goods. The sensitivity of the reaction to the prices is described by the elasticity of transformation. When a UK car company, for example, makes its cars, they would attach more functions to the vehicles exported to Japan responding to Japanese preference. The more changes firms add to their products for export, the more cost is entailed. So, if the quality of products differs greatly between domestic sales and exports, the elasticity of transformation is relatively low.

Products allocated for domestic sales are combined with imported products with a CES function to make a composite commodity for domestic consumers such as household, government, investment, and intermediate inputs for other sectors. It is easier to understand by imagining that a firm mixes long-grain with short-grain rice to sell on the domestic market. If a rice crop failure occurred in a country, the relative price would be changed, raising domestic price, and therefore imported rice is used more to supply for the domestic consumers. Like a CET function, the elasticity of substitution in a CES function implies the similarity of the products between domestic and imported commodities.

The country of the model is assumed to be an open-small country, which suggests that international trades are conducted, but the size of the economy is not large enough to influence the world prices (Equations (2.14.) and (2.15.)). The balance of payments assumes that the export value in foreign currency plus foreign saving is equal to the import value in foreign currency (Equation (2.13.)).

-Gross output transforming firm CET transformation function

$$Z_i = \theta_i \left(\xi_i^e E_i^{\phi_i} + \xi_i^d D_i^{\phi_i} \right)^{1/\phi_i} \qquad \forall i \quad (2.7.)$$

Composite export supply function

$$E_i = \left(\frac{\theta_i^{\phi_i} \xi_i^e \left(1 + \tau_i^z\right) p_i^z}{p_i^e} \right)^{\frac{1}{1-\phi_i}} Z_i \qquad \forall i \quad (2.8.)$$

Domestic good supply function

$$D_i = \left(\frac{\theta_i^{\phi_i} \xi_i^d \left(1 + \tau_i^z\right) p_i^z}{p_i^d} \right)^{\frac{1}{1-\phi_i}} Z_i \qquad \forall i \quad (2.9.)$$

Armington composite good producing firm Composite good production function

$$Q_i = \gamma_i \left(\delta_i^m M_i^{\eta_i} + \delta_i^d D_i^{\eta_i} \right)^{1/\eta_i} \qquad \forall i \quad (2.10.)$$

Composite import demand function

$$M_i = \left(\frac{\gamma_i^{\eta_i} \delta_i^m p_i^q}{(1 + \tau_i^m) p_i^m} \right)^{\frac{1}{1-\eta_i}} Q_i \qquad \forall i \quad (2.11.)$$

Domestic good demand function

$$D_i = \left(\frac{\gamma_i^{\eta_i} \delta_i^d p_i^q}{p_i^d} \right)^{\frac{1}{1-\eta_i}} Q_i \qquad \forall i \quad (2.12.)$$

Balance of payments and export and import price

$$\sum_i p_i^{We} E_i + S^f = \sum_i p_i^{Wm} M_i \qquad (2.13.)$$

$$p_i^e = \varepsilon p_i^{We} \qquad \forall i \quad (2.14.)$$

$$p_i^m = \varepsilon p_i^{Wm} \qquad \forall i \quad (2.15.)$$

Endogenous Variables

Q_i	: Armington composite good
M_i	: composite imports
D_i	: domestic goods
E_i	: composite exports
p_i^m	: price of composite imports
p_i^d	: price of domestic goods
p_i^e	: price of composite exports
ε	: exchange rate

Exogenous Variables

p_i^{Wm}	: world import price
p_i^{We}	: world export price
t_i^z	: domestic production tax rate
t_i^m	: import tax rate
S^f	: current account deficits in US dollars

Parameters

θ_i : scale parameter of transformation function

ξ_i : share parameter of transformation function

σ_i^t : elasticity of transformation

ϕ_i : parameter related to the elasticity of transformation

$$\left(\phi_i = \frac{\sigma_{i\,i}^{t} - 1}{\sigma_i^t} \right)$$

γ_i : scale parameter of Armington composite function

δ_i : share parameter of Armington composite function

σ_i^s : elasticity of substitution for an Armington function

η_i : parameter related to the elasticity of substitution

$$\left(\eta_i = \frac{\sigma_i^s + 1}{\sigma_i^s} \right)$$

Household behaviour (Equation (2.16.)-(2.17.))

The household offers their labour and capital to domestic firms for income, and it consumes goods such as wheat and rice so that it maximises its utility subject to the budget constraint (Equations (2.16.) and (2.17.)). Disposable income for the household is factor payments minus income tax and household saving. In the standard model, the Cobb-Douglas form is assumed, though a CES function is also often applied instead.

-Household

Utility function: $UU = \prod_i X_i^{p\,\alpha_i}$ (2.16.)

Demand functions for consumption

$$X_i^p = \frac{\alpha_i}{p_i^q}\left(\sum_{h,j} p_{h,j}^f F_{h,j} - T^d - S^p \right) \qquad \forall i \quad (2.17.)$$

Endogenous Variables

X_i^p : household consumption

S^p : household savings

T^d : direct taxes

UU : household utility

Parameter

α_i : share parameter of household consumption

Government behaviour (Equation (2.18.)-(2.21.))

The utility function of the government is also assumed to be the Cobb-Douglas form like the household (Equation (2.18.)). Yet, the budget composition is different from that of the household. The budget source of the government is from direct tax, production tax and import tariff, and the disposable income is the tax revenue minus government saving. Direct tax revenue is equal to the income tax rate multiplied by the factor endowments (Equation (2.19.)).The production tax revenue is defined as the domestic production multiplied by the production tax rate (Equation (2.20.)). Import tariff rate is imposed on import goods (Equation (2.21.)). These tax rates are ad valorem.

-Government Demand function for government consumption

$$X_i^g = \frac{\mu_i}{p_i^q}\left(T^d + \sum_j T_j^z + \sum_j T_j^m - S^g\right) \qquad \forall i \qquad (2.18.)$$

Direct tax revenue

$$T^d = \tau^d \sum_h p_h^f FF_h \qquad (2.19.)$$

Production tax revenue

$$T_j^z = \tau_j^z p_j^z Z_j \qquad \forall j \qquad (2.20.)$$

Import tariff revenue

$$T_j^m = \tau_j^m p_j^m M_j \qquad \forall j \qquad (2.21.)$$

Endogenous Variables

X_i^g : government consumption

T_j^z : production taxes

T_j^m : import tariffs

S^g : government savings

Exogenous Variables

τ^d : direct tax rates

τ_i^z : production tax rates

τ_i^m : import tariff rates on inbound shipping from the s-th region

Parameter

μ_i : share parameter of government consumption

Investment behaviour (Equation (2.22.)-(2.24.))

The model is a static, one-period model. This contradicts investment behaviour since investment is, in nature, behaviour for the future. If there is no "next period" in the model, no one should be motivated to save money and invest.

Household allocates the factor payment to saving at a constant rate (Equation (2.23.)), and government also saves at a fixed rate from tax revenue (Equation (2.24.)). Like the household and government behaviour, the Cobb-Douglas function is assumed for the investment behaviour (Equation (2.22.)). The revenue sources for investment are savings by household, government and foreign countries. It is assumed that the investment agent expends the whole revenue on investment purposes. However, it has to be noted that the investment influences neither the utility of household nor the production of firms directly, owing to the nature of the static model.

-Investment Demand function for commodities for investment uses

$$X_i^v = \frac{\lambda_i}{p_i^q}\left(S^p + S^g + \varepsilon\, S^f\right) \qquad \forall i \qquad (2.22.)$$

$$S^p = ss^p \sum_h p_h^f FF_h \qquad (2.23.)$$

$$S_g = ss^g (T^d + \sum_j T_j^z + \sum_j T_j^m) \tag{2.24.}$$

Endogenous Variable

X_i^v : investment uses

Exogenous Variable

$FF_{h,j}$: factor endowment initially employed in the j-th sector

Parameters

λ_i : share parameter of investment

ss^p : average propensity to save for household

ss^g : average propensity to save for government

Market equilibrium conditions (Equation (2.25.)-(2.26.))

We have explained the behaviours of each agent such as household, government, investment, and firms. The demand and supply have to be equalised through the price mechanism (Equation (2.25.)). The supply and demand of production factors are also balanced through the price changes on the markets (Equation (2.26.)).

-Market-clearing conditions Commodity market

$$Q_i = X_i^p + X_i^g + X_i^v + \sum_j X_{i,j} \qquad \forall i \tag{2.25.}$$

Capital and land markets

$$FF_h = \sum_j F_{h,j} \qquad \forall h \tag{2.26.}$$

Calibration

To run the model, scale and share parameters of the equations need to be calculated. We indicate how to estimate the scale and share parameters of the Cobb-Douglas, CES, CET, and Leontief functions below ((2.16.), (2.10.), (2.7.) and (2.3.)). The zero at the top right of the endogenous variables signifies values at the initial equilibrium. In a CGE model, the prices are assumed to be one at the initial equilibrium because all the prices are treated as relative prices not absolute prices in a CGE model. For this, the cell (Production Activities, Household) in Table 2.1 is assigned for X_i^{p0}, and p_i^{q0} is one pound. Namely, X_{wheat}^{p0} and X_{rice}^{p0} are 13 and 18 units, respectively. The one unit means the quantity of wheat/rice he or she can buy for one pound.

$$UU = \prod_i X_i^{p\alpha_i} \qquad (2.16.)$$

$$\alpha_i = \frac{p_i^{q0} X_i^{q0}}{\sum_i p_i^{q0} X_i^{q0}} \qquad \forall i \quad (2.16.1)$$

$$Q_i = \gamma_i \left(\delta_i^m M_i^{\eta_i} + \delta_i^d D_i^{\eta_i}\right)^{1/\eta_i} \qquad \forall i \quad (2.10.)$$

$$\delta_i^m = \frac{(1+\tau_i^{m0}) p_i^{m0} M_i^{0(1-\eta_i)}}{(1+\tau_i^{m0}) p_i^{m0} M_i^{0(1-\eta_i)} + p_i^{d0} D_i^{0(1-\eta_i)}} \qquad \forall i \quad (2.10.1)$$

$$\delta_i^d = \frac{p_i^{d0} D_i^{0(1-\eta_i)}}{(1+\tau_i^{m0}) p_i^{m0} M_i^{0(1-\eta_i)} + p_i^{d0} D_i^{0(1-\eta_i)}} \qquad \forall i \quad (2.10.2)$$

$$\gamma_i = \frac{Q_i^0}{\left(\delta_i^m M_i^{0\eta_i} + \delta_i^d D_i^{0\eta_i}\right)^{1/\eta_i}} \qquad \forall i \quad (2.10.3)$$

$$Z_i = \theta_i \left(\xi_i^e E_i^{\phi_i} + \xi_i^d D_i^{\phi_i}\right)^{1/\phi_i} \qquad \forall i \quad (2.7.)$$

$$\xi_i^e = \frac{p_i^{e0} E_i^{0(1-\phi_i)}}{p_i^{e0} E_i^{0(1-\phi_i)} + p_i^{d0} D_i^{0(1-\phi_i)}} \qquad \forall i \quad (2.7.1)$$

$$\xi_i^d = \frac{p_i^{d0} D_i^{0(1-\phi_i)}}{p_i^{e0} E_i^{0(1-\phi_i)} + p_i^{d0} D_i^{0(1-\phi_i)}} \qquad \forall i \quad (2.7.2)$$

$$\theta_i = \frac{Z_i^0}{\left(\xi_i^e E_i^{\phi_i} + \xi_i^d D_i^{\phi_i}\right)^{1/\phi_i}} \qquad \forall i \quad (2.7.3)$$

$$Z_j = \min\left(\frac{X_{i,j}}{ax_{i,j}}, \frac{Y_j}{ay_j}\right) \qquad \forall j \qquad (2.3.)$$

$$ax_{i,j} = \frac{X_{i,j}^0}{Z_i^0} \qquad \forall i,j \qquad (2.3.1)$$

$$ay_i = \frac{Y_i^0}{Z_i^0} \qquad \forall i \qquad (2.3.2)$$

A standard world CGE model

A single-country CGE model was outlined in the previous section, which will be extended to a world scale. A regional dimension is added to many of the variables of the single-country model like the extension of a SAM of a single-country. However, some variables and equations need to be modified, erased or introduced for an international model.

Figure 2.3 shows the structure of a sector in a world CGE model. The new portions are at export and import. Under the CET technology, domestic production is allocated either to domestic sales or composite exports, which are also distributed to each export destination using a CET function. Similarly, imported goods from each region are aggregated to produce a composite import good with a CES function. Then a composite import is combined with a domestic good for a composite commodity using a CES function. In addition, the world model has a global transport sector though it is not depicted on Figure 2.3.

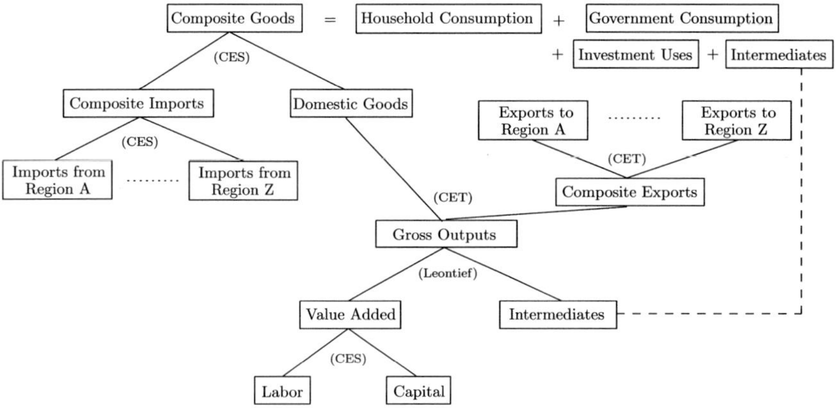

Figure 2.3: The structure of a standard world CGE model

In Equation (2.1.), factor use tax rates, τ_j^{va} , are exchanged for Equation (2.1.'). A transport sector needs to be made for a region to complete the world model since an inter-regional transport sector is introduced. It has economic activities in a domestic market, but also operates the international shipping services. Hence, domestic production $Z_{j,r}$ is subtracted by international freight TT_r (Equations (2.8.') and (2.9.')). While the single-country model assumed that the world prices of export and import are exogenous, they are endogenous in the world model (Equation (2.13.')). On the international markets of the model, it is assumed that all the trade dealings are made in US dollars. Factor use and export taxes are added into the revenue term of government expenditure and saving behaviour equations (Equations (2.18.') and (2.24.')).

Equations to be modified

$$F_{h,j} = \left(\frac{b_j^{\eta_j^{va}} \beta_{h,j} p_j^y}{p_{h,j}^f} \right)^{\frac{1}{1-\eta_j^{va}}} Y_j \qquad \forall j \quad (2.1.)$$

$$E_i = \left(\frac{\theta_i^{\phi_i} \xi_i^e \left(1+\tau_i^z\right) p_i^z}{p_i^e} \right)^{\frac{1}{1-\phi_i}} Z_i \qquad \forall i \quad (2.8.)$$

$$D_i = \left(\frac{\theta_i^{\phi_i} \xi_i^d \left(1+\tau_i^z\right) p_i^z}{p_i^d} \right)^{\frac{1}{1-\phi_i}} Z_i \qquad \forall i \qquad (2.9.)$$

$$\sum_i p_i^{We} E_i + S^f = \sum_i p_i^{Wm} M_i \qquad (2.13.)$$

$$X_i^g = \frac{\mu_i}{p_i^q} \left(T^d + \sum_j T_j^z + \sum_j T_j^m - S^g \right) \qquad \forall i \qquad (2.18.)$$

$$S_g = ss^g (T^d + \sum_j T_j^z + \sum_j T_j^m) \qquad (2.24.)$$

Equations after the modifications

$$F_{h,j,r} = \left(\frac{b_{j,r}{}^{\eta_j^{va}} \beta_{h,j,r} p_{j,r}^y}{\left(1+\tau_{h,j,r}^f\right) p_{h,j,r}^f} \right)^{\frac{1}{1-\eta_j^{va}}} Y_{j,r} \qquad \forall h,j,r \qquad (2.1.')$$

i = transport

$$E_{i,r} = \left(\frac{\theta_{i,r}{}^{\phi_i} \xi_{i,r}^e \left(1+\tau_{i,r}^z\right) p_{i,r}^z}{p_{i,r}^e} \right)^{\frac{1}{1-\phi_i}} \left(Z_{i,r} - TT_r\right) \qquad \forall i,r \qquad (2.8.')$$

$$D_{i,r} = \left(\frac{\theta_{i,r}{}^{\phi_i} \xi_{i,r}^d \left(1+\tau_{i,r}^z\right) p_{i,r}^z}{p_{i,r}^d} \right)^{\frac{1}{1-\phi_i}} \left(Z_{i,r} - TT_r\right) \qquad \forall i,r \qquad (2.9.')$$

$$\sum_{i,s} (1+\tau_{i,r,s}^e) \varepsilon_{r,USA} p_{i,r,s}^t T_{i,r,s} + S_r^f + \varepsilon_{r,USA} (1+\tau_{TRS,r}^z) p_{TRS,r}^z TT_r$$

$$= \sum_{i,s} \left[\tau_{i,s,r}^s p^s \varepsilon_{USA,USA} + (1+\tau_{i,s,r}^e) p_{i,s,r}^t \varepsilon_{s,USA} \right] T_{i,s,r}$$

$$\forall r \qquad (2.13.')$$

$$X_{i,r}^g = \frac{\mu_{i,r}}{p_{i,r}^q} \left(T_r^d + \sum_j T_{j,r}^z + \sum_{j,s} T_{j,s,r}^m + \sum_{j,s} T_{j,r,s}^e + \sum_{h,j} T_{h,j,r}^f - S_r^g \right)$$

$$\forall i,r \qquad (2.18.')$$

$$S_r^g = s_r^g \left(T_r^d + \sum_j T_{j,r}^z + \sum_{j,s} T_{j,s,r}^m + \sum_{j,s} T_{j,r,s}^e + \sum_{h,j} T_{h,j,r}^f \right) \quad \forall r \quad (2.24.')$$

New Set

r, s, r' : regions

New Endogenous Variables

TT_r : exports of inter-regional shipping service by the r-th region

$T_{i,r,s}$: inter-regional transportation from the r-th region to the s-th region

p^s : inter-regional shipping service price in US dollars

$p_{i,r,s}^t$: price of goods shipped from the r-th region to the s-th region

$T_{j,r,s}^e$: export taxes

$T_{h,j,r}^f$: factor input taxes

New Exogenous Variables

$\tau_{h,j,r}^f$: factor input tax rates

$\tau_{i,r,s}^e$: export tax rates on outbound shipping to the s-th region

$\tau_{i,r,s}^s$: inter-regional shipping service requirement per unit transportation of the i-th good from the r-th region to the s-th region

As world price was exogenously given in the single-country model, Equations (2.14.) and (2.15.) are eliminated. As stated above, import and export have a two-steps nested structure (Equations (2.A.25.), (2.A.26.), (2.A.20.), and (2.A.21.)). The exported shipping service of each region is input to produce a global transport composite good (Equations (2.A.28.) and (2.A.29.)), and the composite and the total shipping fee from imports is equalised (Equation (2.A.33.)). Equation (2.A.32.) suggests the consistent relationships among exchange rates.

Removed equations

$$p_i^e = \varepsilon p_i^{We} \qquad \forall i \qquad (2.14.)$$

$$p_i^m = \varepsilon p_i^{Wm} \qquad \forall i \qquad (2.15.)$$

New equations

International trade

$$E_{i,r} = \varsigma_{i,r}\left(\sum_s \rho_{i,r,s} T_{i,r,s}{}^{\varphi_i}\right)^{1/\varphi_i} \qquad \forall i,r \qquad (2.A.25)$$

$$T_{i,r,s} = \left(\frac{\varsigma_{i,r}{}^{\varphi_i}\rho_{i,r,s} p_{i,r}^e}{(1+\tau_{i,r,s}^e)p_{i,r,s}^t}\right)^{\frac{1}{1-\varphi_i}} E_{i,r} \qquad \forall i,r,s \qquad (2.A.26)$$

$$M_{i,r} = \omega_{i,r}\left(\sum_s \kappa_{i,s,r} T_{i,s,r}{}^{\varpi_i}\right)^{1/\varpi_i} \qquad \forall i,r \qquad (2.A.20)$$

$$T_{i,s,r} = \left(\frac{\omega_{i,r}{}^{\varpi_i}\kappa_{i,s,r} p_{i,r}^m}{\left(1+\tau_{i,s,r}^m\right)\left[(1+\tau_{i,s,r}^e)\varepsilon_{s,r} p_{i,s,r}^t + \tau_{i,s,r}^s \varepsilon_{USA,r} p^s\right]}\right)^{\frac{1}{1-\varpi_i}} M_{i,r} \qquad \forall i,s,r \qquad (2.A.21)$$

Global transport sector

$$Q^s = c\prod_r TT_r{}^{\chi_r} \qquad (2.A.28)$$

$$TT_r = \frac{\chi_r}{\left(1+\tau_{TRS,r}^z\right)\,\varepsilon_{r,USA} p_{TRS,r}^z} p^s Q^s \qquad \forall r \qquad (2.A.29)$$

$$Q^s = \sum_{i,r,s} \tau_{i,r,s}^s T_{i,r,s} \qquad (2.A.33)$$

Foreign exchange rate arbitrage condition

$$\varepsilon_{r,r'} \cdot \varepsilon_{r',s} = \varepsilon_{r,s} \qquad \forall r,r',s \qquad (2.A.32)$$

New Parameters

$\zeta_{i,r}$: scale parameter of composite export transformation function

$\rho_{i,r,s}$: share parameter of export

$\omega_{i,r}$: scale parameter of composite import production function

$\kappa_{i,r,s}$: share parameter of import

Standard world CGE model equations

All the equations for the global CGE model explained in the previous section are described below.

-Household

(Utility function: $UU_r = \prod_i X_{i,r}^{p\ \alpha_{i,r}} \quad \forall r$) (2.A.1.)

Demand functions for consumption

$$X_{i,r}^{p} = \frac{\alpha_{i,r}}{p_{i,r}^{q}} \left(\sum_{h,j} p_{h,j,r}^{f} F_{h,j,r} - T_r^d - S_r^p \right) \qquad \forall i,r \qquad (2.A.2.)$$

Savings function

$$S_r^p = s_r^p \sum_{h,j} p_{h,j,r}^{f} F_{h,j,r} \qquad \forall r \qquad (2.A.3.)$$

-Value added producing firm

Factor demand function

$$F_{h,j,r} = \left(\frac{b_{j,r}^{\ \eta_j^{va}} \beta_{h,j,r} p_{j,r}^{y}}{p_{h,j,r}^{f}} \right)^{\frac{1}{1-\eta_j^{va}}} Y_{j,r} \qquad \forall h,j,r \qquad (2.A.4.)$$

Value added production function

$$Y_{j,r} = b_{j,r} \left(\sum_h \beta_{h,j,r} F_{h,j,r}^{\ \eta_j^{va}} \right)^{1/\eta_j^{va}} \qquad \forall j,r \qquad (2.A.5.)$$

-Gross output producing firm

(Production function: $Z_{j,r} = \min\left(\left\{\frac{X_{i,j,r}}{ax_{i,j,r}}\right\}_i, \frac{Y_{j,r}}{ay_{j,r}}\right) \quad \forall j,r$)

(2.A.6.)

Demand function for intermediates

$$X_{i,j,r} = \alpha x_{i,j,r} Z_{j,r} \qquad \forall i,j,r \qquad (2.A.7.)$$

Demand function for value added

$$Y_{j,r} = ay_{j,r} Z_{j,r} \qquad \forall j,r \qquad (2.A.8.)$$

Unit price function

$$p^z_{j,r} = \sum_i ax_{i,j,r} p^q_{i,r} + ay_{j,r} p^y_{j,r} \qquad \forall j,r \qquad (2.A.9.)$$

-Government

Demand function for government consumption

$$X^g_{i,r} = \frac{\mu_{i,r}}{p^q_{i,r}}\left(T^d_r + \sum_j T^z_{j,r} + \sum_{j,s} T^m_{j,s,r} + \sum_{j,s} T^e_{j,r,s} + \sum_{h,j} T^f_{h,j,r} - S^g_r\right) \qquad \forall i,r \qquad (2.A.10.)$$

Direct tax revenue

$$T^d_r = \tau^d_r \sum_{h,j} p^f_{h,j,r} F_{h,j,r} \qquad \forall r \qquad (2.A.11.)$$

Production tax revenue

$$T^z_{j,r} = \tau^z_{j,r} p^z_{j,r} Z_{j,r} \qquad \forall j,r \qquad (2.A.12.)$$

Import tariff revenue

$$T^m_{j,s,r} = \tau^m_{j,s,r}\left[\left(1 + \tau^e_{j,s,r}\right)\varepsilon_{s,r} p^t_{j,s,r} + \tau^s_{j,s,r} \varepsilon_{USA,r} p^s\right] T_{j,s,r} \qquad \forall j,s,r \qquad (2.A.13.)$$

Export tax revenue

$$T^e_{j,r,s} = \tau^e_{j,r,s} p^t_{j,r,s} T_{j,r,s} \qquad \forall j,r,s \qquad (2.A.14.)$$

Government savings function

$$S_r^g = s_r^g \left(T_r^d + \sum_j T_{j,r}^z + \sum_{j,s} T_{j,s,r}^m + \sum_{j,s} T_{j,r,s}^e + \sum_{h,j} T_{h,j,r}^f \right) \qquad \forall r \qquad (2.A.15.)$$

-Investment

Demand function for commodities for investment uses

$$X_{i,r}^v = \frac{\lambda_{i,r}}{p_{i,r}^q} \left(S_r^p + S_r^g + \varepsilon_{USA,r} S_r^f \right) \qquad \forall i,r \qquad (2.A.16.)$$

-Armington composite good producing firm

Composite good production function

$$Q_{i,r} = \gamma_{i,r} \left(\delta_{i,r}^m M_{i,r}{}^{\eta_i} + \delta_{i,r}^d D_{i,r}{}^{\eta_i} \right)^{1/\eta_i} \qquad \forall i,r \qquad (2.A.17.)$$

Composite import demand function

$$M_{i,r} = \left(\frac{\gamma_{i,r}{}^{\eta_i} \delta_{i,r}^m p_{i,r}^q}{p_{i,r}^m} \right)^{\frac{1}{1-\eta_i}} Q_{i,r} \qquad \forall i,r \qquad (2.A.18.)$$

Domestic good demand function

$$D_{i,r} = \left(\frac{\gamma_{i,r}{}^{\eta_i} \delta_{i,r}^d p_{i,r}^q}{p_{i,r}^d} \right)^{\frac{1}{1-\eta_i}} Q_{i,r} \qquad \forall i,r \qquad (2.A.19.)$$

-Import variety aggregation firm

Composite import production function

$$M_{i,r} = \omega_{i,r} \left(\sum_s \kappa_{i,s,r} T_{i,s,r}{}^{\varpi_i} \right)^{1/\varpi_i} \qquad \forall i,r \qquad (2.A.20.)$$

Import demand function

$$T_{i,s,r} = \left(\frac{\omega_{i,r}{}^{\varpi_i} \kappa_{i,s,r} p_{i,r}^m}{\left(1+\tau_{i,s,r}^m\right)\left[\left(1+\tau_{i,s,r}^e\right)\varepsilon_{s,r} p_{i,s,r}^t + \tau_{i,s,r}^s \varepsilon_{USA,r} p^s\right]} \right)^{\frac{1}{1-\varpi_i}} M_{i,r} \qquad \forall i,s,r \qquad (2.A.21.)$$

-Gross output transforming firm

$$Z_{i,r} = \theta_{i,r}\left(\xi^{e}_{i,r} {E_{i,r}}^{\phi_i} + \xi^{d}_{i,r} {D_{i,r}}^{\phi_i}\right)^{1/\phi_i} \qquad \forall i,r \qquad (2.A.22.)$$

$$E_{i,r} = \left(\frac{{\theta_{i,r}}^{\phi_i}\xi^{e}_{i,r}\left(1+\tau^{z}_{i,r}\right)p^{z}_{i,r}}{p^{e}_{i,r}}\right)^{\frac{1}{1-\phi_i}} Z_{i,r} \qquad \forall i,r \qquad (2.A.23.)$$

$$D_{i,r} = \left(\frac{{\theta_{i,r}}^{\phi_i}\xi^{d}_{i,r}\left(1+\tau^{z}_{i,r}\right)p^{z}_{i,r}}{p^{d}_{i,r}}\right)^{\frac{1}{1-\phi_i}} Z_{i,r} \qquad \forall i,r \qquad (2.A.24.)$$

-Export variety producing firm

Composite export transformation function

$$E_{i,r} = \varsigma_{i,r}\left(\sum_{s}\rho_{i,r,s}{T_{i,r,s}}^{\varphi_i}\right)^{1/\varphi_i} \qquad \forall i,r \qquad (2.A.25.)$$

Export supply function

$$T_{i,r,s} = \left(\frac{{\varsigma_{i,r}}^{\varphi_i}\rho_{i,r,s}p^{e}_{i,r}}{p^{t}_{i,r,s}}\right)^{\frac{1}{1-\varphi_i}} E_{i,r} \qquad \forall i,r,s \qquad (2.A.26.)$$

Balance of payments

$$\sum_{i,s}(1+\tau^{e}_{i,r,s})\varepsilon_{r,USA}\,p^{t}_{i,r,s}T_{i,r,s} + S^{f}_{r} + \varepsilon_{r,USA}(1+\tau^{z}_{TRS,r})\,p^{z}_{TRS,r}TT_{r}$$

$$= \sum_{i,s}\left[\tau^{s}_{i,s,r}\,p^{s}\varepsilon_{USA,USA} + (1+\tau^{e}_{i,s,r})\,p^{t}_{i,s,r}\varepsilon_{s,USA}\right]T_{i,s,r}$$

$$\forall r \qquad (2.A.27.)$$

-Inter-regional shipping sector

Inter-regional shipping service production function

$$Q^{s} = c\prod_{r}{TT_{r}}^{\chi_r} \qquad (2.A.28.)$$

Input demand function for international shipping service provided by the r-th country

$$TT_r = \frac{\chi_r}{\left(1+\tau^z_{TRS,r}\right)\ \varepsilon_{r,USA}\, p^z_{TRS,r}} p^s Q^s \qquad \forall r \qquad (2.A.29.)$$

-Market-clearing conditions
Commodity market

$$Q_{i,r} = X^p_{i,r} + X^g_{i,r} + X^v_{i,r} + \sum_j X_{i,j,r} \qquad \forall i,r \qquad (2.A.30.)$$

Capital and land markets

$$FF_{h,r} = \sum_j F_{h,j,r} \qquad \forall h,r \qquad (2.A.31.)$$

Foreign exchange rate arbitrage condition

$$\varepsilon_{r,r'} \cdot \varepsilon_{r',s} = \varepsilon_{r,s} \qquad \forall r,r',s \qquad (2.A.32.)$$

Inter-regional shipping service market

$$Q^s = \sum_{i,r,s} \tau^s_{i,r,s} T_{i,r,s} \qquad (2.A.33.)$$

The modification of the standard CGE model for Chapter 3

Chapter 3 will discuss rice trade liberalisation policy by Japan. This section describes how the standard world CGE model is changed for Chapter 3.

The Monte Carlo method[9]

While some countries call on Japan's government to abolish the import tariff on rice, the government has refused the proposal primarily on the ground of its food security. Several papers have evaluated the impacts of the rice free trade on its economy. Yet, most focus on the deterministic effects, and therefore do not clearly answer whether the nation could secure its food supply in an emergency after liberalisation. Chapter 3 will

[9] This section explains the Monte Carlo method in general. For more information see Miyatake and Nakayama (1960). Specific information on the method for this book will be described in Chapter 3.

try to contribute to this by assessing the probabilistic impacts of the rice trade liberalisation, using an application of the Monte Carlo method taking into consideration the rice productivity shocks of all the regions.

The Monte Carlo method is an approach to solve deterministic or probabilistic mathematical problems using random numbers. Probabilistic problems are simulations of a probabilistic phenomenon (or phenomena). In the simulation, the elements are partly or entirely probabilistic, and the probability of the events has to be specified. Deterministic problems are where the problem is analytically solvable, but the equations are too complex to solve or calculation efforts are enormous. The research in Chapter 3 is the former classification and solves stochastic phenomena (possible welfare or consumption changes of household) by generating random rice productivity shocks.

It originates from an idea by an American mathematician from Poland, Stanislaw Marcin Ulam, who worked for the Los Alamos Laboratory around 1946 (Metropolis and Ulam, 1949). It is said that Ulam was thinking of the probability for finishing the card game "Solitaire." The calculation efforts are huge for the exponential increase in combination, but he realised and told John von Neumann that the probability could be approximated by randomly repeating the game, and that this method could also be applied to explaining the diffusional phenomenon of the neutron in nuclear materials. They devised the method of generating pseudo-random numbers on a computer and so transforming a deterministic problem to a probabilistic model.

As mentioned, an advantage of the Monte Carlo method is to make it possible to approximate the solution of a problem that is not analytically solvable. On the other hand, one of the disadvantages is not to be able to avoid an error for a solution. Further, lots of experiments need to be conducted for the high precision of estimation.

Productivity shocks parameter of paddy rice sector

In Chapter 3, a paddy rice productivity parameter is introduced into a domestic rice production function (Equation (2.A.6.)), and thereby Equations (2.A.7.), (2.A.8.) and (2.A.9.) are also transformed into Equations ((2.A.6.'), (2.A.7.'), (2.A.8.') and (2.A.9.')).

Equations after modification

$$Z_{j,r} = TFP_{j,r} \min\left(\left\{ \frac{X_{i,j,r}}{ax_{i,j,r}} \right\}_i , \frac{Y_{j,r}}{ay_{j,r}} \right) \qquad \forall j,r \qquad (2.A.6.')$$

$$X_{i,j,r} = \frac{\alpha x_{i,j,r} Z_{j,r}}{TFP_{j,r}} \qquad \forall i,j,r \qquad (2.A.7.')$$

$$Y_{j,r} = \frac{ay_{j,r} Z_{j,r}}{TFP_{j,r}} \qquad \forall j,r \qquad (2.A.8.')$$

$$p^z_{j,r} = \frac{1}{TFP_{j,r}} \left(\sum_i ax_{i,j,r} p^q_{i,r} + ay_{j,r} p^y_{j,r} \right) \qquad \forall j,r \qquad (2.A.9.')$$

New exogenous variable

$TFP_{j,r}$: productivity of j-th sector in r-th region (used only in rice sector)

Emergency rice stock

Chapter 3 will also simulate the effectiveness of a rice buffer stock in Japan. A rice stock variable is inserted into Equations (2.A.22.), (2.A.23.) and (2.A.24.), which are replacing Equations (2.A.22.'), (2.A.23.'), and (2.A.24.'). Equation (2.A.34.) expresses that rice stock is released into markets only when a rice productivity shock is negative.

Equations after modification

$$Z_{i,r} + EMS_r = \theta_{i,r} \left(\xi^e_{i,r} E_{i,r}^{\phi_i} + \xi^d_{i,r} D_{i,r}^{\phi_i} \right)^{1/\phi_i} \qquad \forall i,r \qquad (2.A.22.')$$

$$E_{i,r} = \left(\frac{\theta_{i,r}^{\phi_i} \xi^e_{i,r} \left(1 + \tau^z_{i,r}\right) p^z_{i,r}}{p^e_{i,r}} \right)^{\frac{1}{1-\phi_i}} \left(Z_{i,r} + EMS_r \right) \qquad \forall i,r \qquad (2.A.23.')$$

$$D_{i,r} = \left(\frac{\theta_{i,r}^{\phi_i} \xi^d_{i,r} \left(1 + \tau^z_{i,r}\right) p^z_{i,r}}{p^d_{i,r}} \right)^{\frac{1}{1-\phi_i}} \left(Z_{i,r} + EMS_r \right) \qquad \forall i,r \qquad (2.A.24.')$$

New equation

$$EMS_r = \min \left(\overline{EMS}_r , \max \left((1 - TFP_{i,r}) Z^0_{i,r} , 0 \right) \right) \qquad r = Japan \qquad (2.A.34.)$$

New endogenous variable

EMS_r : releases of emergency rice stock

New exogenous variable

$\overline{EMS}_r$: the capacity of emergency rice stock

Export restrictions

To evaluate the impacts of export restrictions on paddy and processed rice to Japan by the US, Thailand, China and Australia, Equations (2.A.35.), (2.A.36.), and (2.A.37.) are added. Trade quantity is reduced by export quota (Equation (2.A.35.)). Equation (2.A.36.) suggests the complementary condition of export quotas. The export quantity is limited by putting rent $\tau^{eq}_{i,r,s}$ on the export price, and its revenue goes to the governmental budget (Equations (2.A.37.), (2.A.10.') and (2.A.15.')). Equations (2.A.21.) and (2.A.27.) are also replaced with rent for (2.A.21.') and (2.A.27.'), respectively.

$$T_{i,r,s} \le EQ_{i,r,s} \qquad \forall i,r \qquad (2.A.35.)$$

$$(T_{i,r,s} - EQ_{i,r,s})\tau^{eq}_{i,r,s} = 0 \qquad \forall i,r \qquad (2.A.36.)$$

$$T^{eq}_{i,r,s} = \tau^{eq}_{i,r,s} p^{t}_{i,r,s} T_{i,r,s} \qquad \forall i,r \qquad (2.A.37.)$$

$$X^{g}_{i,r} = \frac{\mu_{i,r}}{p^{q}_{i,r}}\left(T^{d}_{r} + \sum_{j} T^{z}_{j,r} + \sum_{j,s} T^{m}_{j,s,r} + \sum_{j,s} T^{e}_{j,r,s} + \sum_{h,j} T^{f}_{h,j,r} + \sum_{j,s} T^{eq}_{j,r,s} - S^{g}_{r}\right) \qquad \forall i,r \qquad (2.A.10.')$$

$$S^{g}_{r} = s^{g}_{r}\left(T^{d}_{r} + \sum_{j} T^{z}_{j,r} + \sum_{j,s} T^{m}_{j,s,r} + \sum_{j,s} T^{e}_{j,r,s} + \sum_{h,j} T^{f}_{h,j,r} + \sum_{j,s} T^{eq}_{j,r,s}\right) \qquad \forall r \qquad (2.A.15.')$$

$$T_{i,s,r} = \left(\frac{\omega_{i,r}^{\ \varpi_i} \kappa_{i,s,r} p_{i,r}^m}{\left(1+\tau_{i,s,r}^m\right)\left[\left(1+\tau_{i,s,r}^e+\tau_{i,s,r}^{eq}\right)\varepsilon_{s,r} p_{i,s,r}^t + \tau_{i,s,r}^s \varepsilon_{USA,r} p^s\right]} \right)^{\frac{1}{1-\varpi_i}} M_{i,r}$$

$$\forall i,r \qquad (2.A.21.')$$

$$\sum_{i,s} (1+\tau_{i,r,s}^e+\tau_{i,r,s}^{eq})\varepsilon_{r,USA} p_{i,r,s}^t T_{i,r,s} + S_r^f + \varepsilon_{r,USA}(1+\tau_{TRS,r}^z) p_{TRS,r}^z TT_r$$

$$= \sum_{i,s} \left[\tau_{i,s,r}^s p^s \varepsilon_{USA,USA} + (1+\tau_{i,s,r}^e+\tau_{i,r,s}^{eq}) p_{i,s,r}^t \varepsilon_{s,USA}\right] T_{i,s,r}$$

$$\forall r \qquad (2.A.27.')$$

New endogenous variable

$T_{i,r,s}^{eq}$: revenue from rent of export restrictions of i-th good from r-th to s-th country

$\tau_{i,r,s}^{eq}$: rent of export restrictions of i-th good from r-th to s-th country

New exogenous variable

$EQ_{i,r,s}$: export quota of i-th good from r-th to s-th country

The structure of household consumption

The Cobb-Douglas form was applied to household consumption in the standard model, but the empirical studies in Chapters 3, 4, 5 and 6 employ a two-steps nested consumption structure for agricultural and food sectors with a CES function (Figure 2.4).

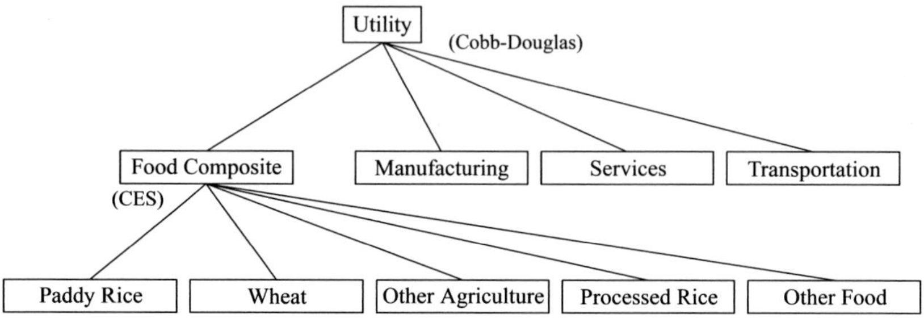

Figure 2.4: the structure of household consumption for Chapter 3

A food composite is put into the utility function (Equation (2.A.1.')), and its demand function for food composite is derived (Equation (2.A.38)). The food composite production function is the CES form (Equations (2.A.39.) and (2.A.40.)).

Utility function for household

$$UU_r = XFD_r^{\alpha_r^{XFD}} \prod_{nfd} X_{nfd,r}^{p\ \ \alpha_{nfd,r}} \qquad \forall r \qquad (2.A.1.')$$

Demand functions for consumption

$$X_{nfd,r}^{p} = \frac{\alpha_{nfd,r}}{p_{nfd,r}^{q}} \left(\sum_{h,j} p_{h,j,r}^{f} F_{h,j,r} - T_r^d - S_r^p \right) \qquad \forall nfd, r \qquad (2.A.2.')$$

$$XFD_r = \frac{\alpha_r^{XFD}}{p_r^{XFD}} \left(\sum_{h,j} p_{h,j,r}^{f} F_{h,j,r} - T_r^d - S_r^p \right) \qquad \forall r \qquad (2.A.38.)$$

Food composite aggregation function

$$XFD_r = \Theta_r \left(\sum_{fd} \Delta_{fd,r} X_{fd,r}^{p\ \ \Psi} \right)^{1/\Psi} \qquad \forall r \qquad (2.A.39.)$$

(Note that $\Psi = (\varepsilon^f - 1)/\varepsilon^f$.)

$$X^{p}_{fd,r} = \left(\frac{\Theta_r^{\Psi} \Delta_{fd,r} p_r^{XFD}}{p^{q}_{fd,r}} \right)^{\frac{1}{1-\Psi}} XFD_r \qquad \forall fd,r \qquad (2.A.40.)$$

New set

fd : agricultural and food sectors

nfd : non-agricultural and food sectors

New endogenous variables

XFD_r : food composite

p_r^{XFD} : price of food composite

New parameters

α_r^{XFD} : share parameter of a food composite

Θ_r : scale parameter of food composite aggregate function

$\Delta_{fd,r}$: share parameter of food composite function

ε^{f} : elasticity of substitution for food

Ψ : parameter related to elasticity of substitution for food

The modification of the standard CGE model for Chapters 4, 5 and 6

Like Chapter 3, the empirical research in Chapters 4, 5, and 6 will employ a world model, part of which is modified from the standard model shown above. The structure of household food consumption and the equations for productivity shocks and export restrictions for Chapter 3 are used in Chapters 4, 5 and 6 too. The new equations for these chapters are world oil price and biofuel production. In addition, energy substitution structures are put into both the firm production and the household consumption.

World oil price

i = oil

$$\sum_r \left[\sum_s \left\{ \varepsilon_{r,usa}(1+\tau_i^o)(1+\tau_{i,r,s}^e+\tau_{i,r,s}^{eq})p_{i,r,s}^t T_{i,r,s} \right\} wgt_{i,r} \right]$$

$$= \sum_r \left[\sum_s \left\{ \varepsilon_{r,usa}(1+\tau_i^o)(1+\tau_{i,r,s}^e+\tau_{i,r,s}^{eq})p_{i,r,s}^t T_{i,r,s} \right\} wgt_{i,r} \right] WOP$$

$$\forall i \quad (2.A.41.)$$

$$T_r^o = \sum_{i,s} \tau_i^o (1+\tau_{i,r,s}^e+\tau_{i,r,s}^{eq})p_{i,r,s}^t T_{i,r,s}$$

$$\forall r \quad (2.A.42.)$$

$$T_{i,s,r} = \left(\frac{\omega_{i,r}{}^{\varpi_i} \kappa_{i,s,r} p_{i,r}^m}{(1+\tau_{i,s,r}^m)\left[(1+\tau_i^o)(1+\tau_{i,s,r}^e+\tau_{i,s,r}^{eq})\varepsilon_{s,r} p_{i,s,r}^t + \tau_{i,s,r}^s \varepsilon_{USA,r} p^s\right]} \right)^{\frac{1}{1-\varpi_i}} M_{i,r}$$

$$\forall i,s,r \quad (2.A.21.")$$

$$\sum_{i,s}(1+\tau_i^o)(1+\tau_{i,r,s}^e+\tau_{i,r,s}^{eq})\varepsilon_{r,USA} p_{i,r,s}^t T_{i,r,s} + S_r^f + \varepsilon_{r,USA}(1+\tau_{TRS,r}^z)p_{TRS,r}^z TT_r$$

$$= \sum_{i,s}\left[\tau_{i,s,r}^s p^s \varepsilon_{USA,USA} + (1+\tau_i^o)(1+\tau_{i,s,r}^e+\tau_{i,r,s}^{eq})p_{i,s,r}^t \varepsilon_{s,USA}\right] T_{i,s,r}$$

$$\forall r \quad (2.A.27.")$$

New endogenous variables

τ_i^o : rent for world oil price

T_r^o : revenue from oil price rent

New exogenous variable

WOP : world oil price control variable

New parameter

$wgt_{i,r}$: export weight

Biofuel production

To measure the impacts of the biofuel production increase in recent years, the sector is subsidised to meet the production targets. In a similar way to the export restriction equations, the domestic production is pushed up by an exogenous variable $PT_{j,r}$ (Equation (2.A.43.)). Equation (2.A.44.) is the complimentary condition for biofuel production. The expenditure is considered in the governmental revenue (Equations (2.A.10.") and (2.A.15.")). The changes are reflected in the supply functions of an export composite and domestic good (Equations (2.A.23.') and (2.A.24.')).

$$Z_{j,r} \geq PT_{j,r} \qquad \forall i,r \qquad (2.A.43.)$$

$$(Z_{j,r} - PT_{j,r})\tau_{j,r}^{pt} = 0 \qquad \forall i,r \qquad (2.A.44.)$$

$$T_{j,r}^{pt} = \tau_{j,r}^{pt} p_{j,r}^{z} Z_{j,r} \qquad \forall i,r \qquad (2.A.45.)$$

$$X_{i,r}^{g} = \frac{\mu_{i,r}}{p_{i,r}^{q}}\left(T_r^d + \sum_j T_{j,r}^z + \sum_{j,s} T_{j,s,r}^m + \sum_{j,s} T_{j,r,s}^e + \sum_{h,j} T_{h,j,r}^f + \sum_{j,s} T_{j,r,s}^{eq} + T_r^o - \sum_j T_{j,r}^{pt} - S_r^g\right) \qquad \forall i,r \qquad (2.A.10.")$$

$$S_r^g = s_r^g\left(T_r^d + \sum_j T_{j,r}^z + \sum_{j,s} T_{j,s,r}^m + \sum_{j,s} T_{j,r,s}^e + \sum_{h,j} T_{h,j,r}^f + \sum_{j,s} T_{j,r,s}^{eq} + T_r^o - \sum_j T_{j,r}^{pt}\right) \qquad \forall r \qquad (2.A.15.")$$

$$E_{i,r} = \left(\frac{\theta_{i,r}^{\phi_i} \xi_{i,r}^{e}\left(1 + \tau_{i,r}^{z} + \tau_{i,r}^{pt}\right)p_{i,r}^{z}}{p_{i,r}^{e}}\right)^{\frac{1}{1-\phi_i}} Z_{i,r} \qquad \forall i,r \qquad (2.A.23.')$$

$$D_{i,r} = \left(\frac{\theta_{i,r}^{\phi_i} \xi_{i,r}^{d}\left(1 + \tau_{i,r}^{z} + \tau_{i,r}^{pt}\right)p_{i,r}^{z}}{p_{i,r}^{d}}\right)^{\frac{1}{1-\phi_i}} Z_{i,r} \qquad \forall i,r \qquad (2.A.24.')$$

New endogenous variables

$\tau_{j,r}^{pt}$: subsidy rate of biofuel production target

$T_{j,r}^{pt}$: subsidy of biofuel production target

New exogenous variable

$PT_{j,r}$: biofuel production target

Energy substitution structure

Figures 2.5 and 2.6 indicate the structure of the model in Chapters 4, 5 and 6. Both the demand and supply sides have the same structure for energy substitution. At the first stage, liquid energy goods such as oil are inputted to produce a liquid energy composite good with a CES function (Equations (2.A.49.), (2.A.50.), (2.A.56.) and (2.A.57.)), which is used to make an energy composite with non-liquid energy goods like coal under the Cobb-Douglas technology (Equations (2.A.46.), (2.A.47.), (2.A.53.), (2.A.54.) and (2.A.55.)). With an energy composite good inserted as an intermediate good, the Leontief domestic production function is transformed to Equation (2.A.6."), and its demand function is derived (Equation (2.A.51.)). The household utility function is also changed adding an energy composite good (Equation (2.A.1.")), and its demand function is Equation (2.A.52.).

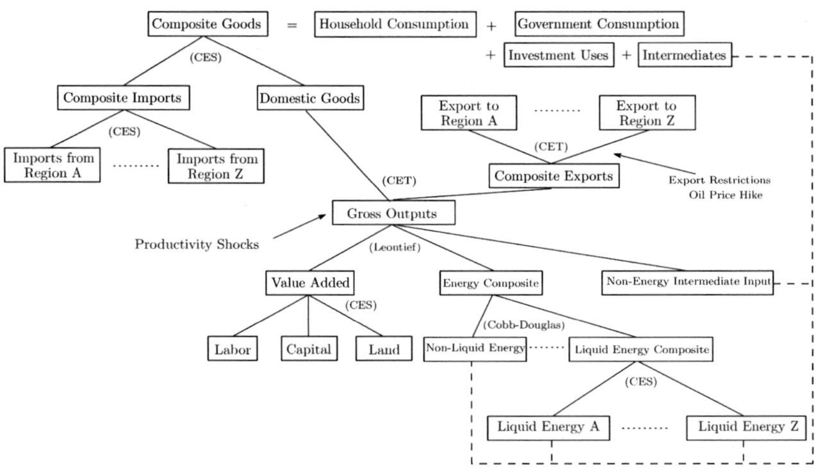

Figure 2.5: Model structure in Chapters 4, 5 and 6.

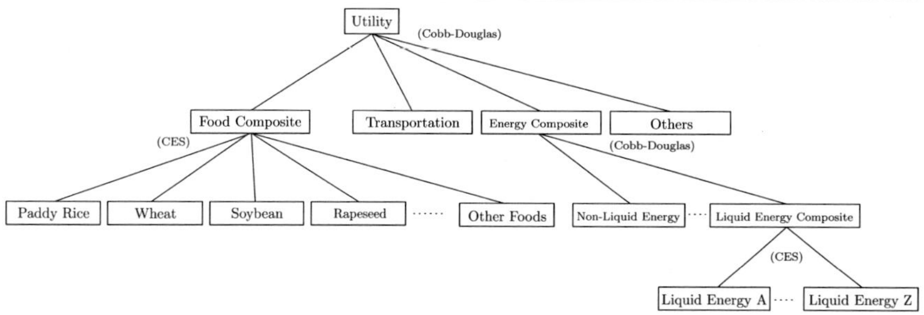

Figure 2.6: Model structure of household consumption in Chapters 4, 5 and 6.

Energy composite aggregation function

$$EC_{j,r} = b_{j,r}^{EC}\left(\prod_{nlq} X_{nlq,j,r}^{\beta_{nlq,j,r}^{EC\_X}}\right) \times LQ_{j,r}^{\beta_{j,r}^{EC\_LQ}} \qquad \forall j,r \qquad (2.A.46.)$$

$$X_{nlq,j,r} = \frac{\beta_{nlq,j,r}^{EC\_X}}{p_{j,r}^{q}} p_{j,r}^{ec} EC_{j,r} \qquad \forall nlq,j,r \qquad (2.A.47.)$$

$$LQ_{j,r} = \frac{\beta_{j,r}^{EC\_LQ}}{p_{j,r}^{lq}} p_{j,r}^{ec} EC_{j,r} \qquad \forall j,r \qquad (2.A.48.)$$

Liquid fuel composite aggregation function

$$LQ_{j,r} = b_{j,r}^{LQ}\left(\sum_{lq} \beta_{lq,j,r}^{LQ} X_{lq,j,r}{}^{\hbar}\right)^{1/\hbar} \qquad \forall j,r \qquad (2.A.49.)$$

(Note that $\hbar = (\sigma^{lq} - 1)/\sigma^{lq}$.)

$$X_{lq,j,r} = \left(\frac{b_{j,r}^{LQ^{\hbar}} \beta_{lq,j,r}^{LQ} p_{j,r}^{lq}}{p_{lq,j,r}^{q}}\right)^{\frac{1}{1-\hbar}} LQ_{j,r} \qquad \forall lq,j,r \qquad (2.A.50.)$$

Gross output producing firm

(Production function: $Z_{j,r} = TFP_{j,r} \min\left(\left\{\frac{X_{nen,j,r}}{ax_{nen,j,r}}\right\}_i, \frac{Y_{j,r}}{ay_{j,r}}, \frac{EC_{j,r}}{aec_{j,r}}\right) \quad \forall j,r$)

(2.A.6.")

$$EC_{j,r} = \frac{aec_{j,r} Z_{j,r}}{TFP_{j,r}} \qquad \forall j,r \qquad (2.A.51.)$$

-Household

$$UU_r = XFD_r^{\alpha_r^{XFD}} \times ECH_r^{\alpha_r^{ECH}} \times \prod_{fd} X_{fd,r}^{p\ \alpha_{fd,r}} \qquad \forall r \qquad (2.A.1.")$$

$$ECH_r = \frac{\alpha_r^{ECH}}{p_r^{ech}} \left(\sum_{h,j} p_{h,j,r}^f F_{h,j,r} - T_r^d - S_r^p \right) \qquad \forall r \qquad (2.A.52.)$$

Energy composite aggregation function for household

$$ECH_r = b_r^{ECH} \left(\prod_{nlq} X_{nlq}^{p\ \beta_{nlq,r}^{ECH}} \times LQH_r^{\beta_r^{LQHC}} \right) \forall r \qquad (2.A.53.)$$

$$X_{nlq,r}^p = \frac{\beta_{nlq,r}^{ECH}}{p_{nlq,r}^q} p_r^{ech} ECH_r \qquad \forall nlq,r \qquad (2.A.54.)$$

$$LQH_r = \frac{\beta_r^{LQHC}}{p_r^{lqh}} p_r^{ech} ECH_r \qquad \forall r \qquad (2.A.55.)$$

Liquid fuel composite aggregation function for household

$$LQH_r = b_r^{LQH} \left(\sum_{lq} \beta_{lq,r}^{LQH} X_{lq,r}^{p\ \Xi} \right)^{1/\Xi} \qquad \forall r \qquad (2.A.56.)$$

(Note that $\Xi = (\sigma^{lqh} - 1)/\sigma^{lqh}$.)

$$X^{p}_{lq,r} = \left(\frac{ {b^{LQH}_{r}}^{\Xi} \beta^{LQH}_{lq,r} \, p^{lqh}_{r} }{ p^{q}_{lq,r} } \right)^{\frac{1}{1-\Xi}} LQH_{r} \qquad \forall lq,r \qquad (2.A.57.)$$

New sets

lq : liquid energy goods

nlq : non-liquid energy goods

New endogenous variables

ECH_{r} : energy composite good for household

LQH_{r} : liquid energy composite good for household

$EC_{j,r}$: energy composite good

$LQ_{j,r}$: liquid energy composite good

$p^{ec}_{j,r}$: price of energy composite good

$p^{lq}_{j,r}$: price of liquid fuel composite good

p^{ech}_{r} : price of energy composite good for household

p^{lqh}_{r} : price of liquid fuel for household

New parameters

$b^{EC}_{j,r}$: scale parameter of energy composite production function

$\beta^{EC\_X}_{nlq,j,r}$: share parameter of a non-liquid energy good for energy composite production function

$\beta^{EC\_LQ}_{j,r}$: share parameter of a liquid energy composite for energy composite production function

$b^{LQ}_{j,r}$: scale parameter of a liquid energy composite production function

$\beta^{LQ}_{lq,j,r}$: share parameter of a liquid energy good for a liquid energy composite production function

$aec_{j,r}$: share parameter of an energy composite good for a domestic production function

α_r^{ECH} : share parameter of an energy composite good for a household utility function

$\beta_{nlq,r}^{ECH}$: share parameter of a non-liquid energy good for a household's energy composite production function

β_r^{LQHC} : share parameter of a liquid energy composite for a household's energy composite production function

b_r^{ECH} : scale parameter of a household's energy composite production function

$\beta_{lq,r}^{LQH}$: share parameter of a liquid energy good for a household's liquid energy composite production function

b_r^{LQH} : scale parameter of a household's liquid energy composite production function

σ^{lq} : elasticity of substitution of liquid energy goods

$\hbar$: parameter related to elasticity of substitution of liquid energy goods

σ^{lqh} :elasticity of substitution of liquid energy goods for household

Ξ : parameter related to elasticity of substitution of liquid energy goods for household

Conclusion

We gave the basics of a SAM and CGE model, and showed our original methods, models and the application of the Monte Carlo method for the book. In the next chapter, we will apply the model to the topic of a rice free trade problem in Japan in order to discuss its food security.

Appendix: list of variables and parameters

The endogenous variables, exogenous variables and parameters of the world standard CGE model, the ones for the empirical studies in the book are listed below.

World standard CGE model
Endogenous variables

$X_{i,r}^{p}$	: household consumption
$X_{i,r}^{g}$	: government consumption
$X_{i,r}^{v}$	: investment uses
$X_{i,j,r}$	: intermediate uses of the i-th good by the j-th sector
$F_{h,j,r}$	: factor uses
$Y_{j,r}$	: value added
$Z_{j,r}$	: gross output
$Q_{i,r}$	: Armington composite good
$M_{i,r}$	: composite imports
$D_{i,r}$	: domestic goods
$E_{i,r}$	: composite exports
$T_{i,r,s}$	: inter-regional transportation from the r-th region to the s-th region
TT_{r}	: exports of inter-regional shipping service by the r-th region
Q^{s}	: composite inter-regional shipping service
S_{r}^{p}	: household savings
S_{r}^{g}	: government savings
T_{r}^{d}	: direct taxes

$T^{z}_{j,r}$: production taxes

$T^{m}_{j,s,r}$: import tariffs

$T^{e}_{j,r,s}$: export taxes

$T^{f}_{h,j,r}$: factor input taxes

$p^{q}_{i,r}$: price of Armington composite goods

$p^{f}_{h,j,r}$: price of factors

$p^{y}_{j,r}$: price of value added

$p^{z}_{i,r}$: price of gross output

$p^{m}_{i,r}$: price of composite imports

$p^{d}_{i,r}$: price of domestic goods

$p^{e}_{i,r}$: price of composite exports

$p^{t}_{i,r,s}$: price of goods shipped from the r-th region to the s-th region

p^{s} : inter-regional shipping service price in US dollars

$\varepsilon_{r,s}$: exchange rates to convert the r-th region's currency into the s-th region's currency

Exogenous variables and parameters

S^{f}_{r} : current account deficits in US dollars

$FF_{h,j,r}$: factor endowment initially employed in the j-th sector

$Z^{0}_{j,r}$: initial amount of gross output

τ^{d}_{r} : direct tax rates

$\tau^{z}_{i,r}$: production tax rates

$\tau^{m}_{i,s,r}$: import tariff rates on inbound shipping from the s-th region

$\tau^{e}_{i,r,s}$: export tax rates on outbound shipping to the s-th region

$\tau^{s}_{i,r,s}$: inter-regional shipping service requirement per unittransportation of the i-th good from the r-th region to the s-th region

$\tau^{f}_{h,j,r}$: factor input tax rates

Parameters

$b_{j,r}$: scale parameter of production function for Yj

$\beta_{h,j,r}$: share parameter of factor input

σ^{f}_{j} : elasticity of substitution for a value added composite function

$ax_{i,j,r}$: share parameter of intermediate input for domestic production

$ay_{j,r}$: share parameter of composite factor input for domestic production

η^{va}_{j} : elasticity parameter $\left(\eta^{va}_{j} = \dfrac{\sigma^{f}_{j} + 1}{\sigma^{f}_{j}}\right)$

$\theta_{i,r}$: scale parameter of transformation function

$\xi_{i,r}$: share parameter of transformation function

σ^{t}_{i} : elasticity of transformation

ϕ_{i} : parameter related to the elasticity of transformation $\left(\phi_{i} = \dfrac{\sigma^{t}_{i\,i} - 1}{\sigma^{t}_{i}}\right)$

$\gamma_{i,r}$: scale parameter of Armington composite function

$\delta_{i,r}$: share parameter of Armington composite function

σ_i^s : elasticity of substitution for an Armington function

η_i : parameter related to the elasticity of substitution $\left(\eta_i = \dfrac{\sigma_i^s + 1}{\sigma_i^s}\right)$

$\zeta_{i,r}$: scale parameter of composite export transformation function

$\rho_{i,r,s}$: share parameter of export

$\omega_{i,r}$: scale parameter of composite import production function

$\kappa_{i,r,s}$: share parameter of import

$\alpha_{i,r}$: share parameter of household consumption

$\mu_{i,r}$: share parameter of government consumption

$\lambda_{i,r}$: share parameter of investment

ss_r^p : average propensity to save for household

ss_r^p : average propensity to save for government

Chapter 3

Endogenous variables

XFD_r : food composite

p_r^{XFD} : price of food composite

EMS_r : release of emergency rice stocks

$T_{i,r,s}^{eq}$: revenue from rent of export restrictions of i-th good from r-th to s-th country

$\tau^{eq}_{i,r,s}$: rent of export restrictions of i-th good from r-th to s-th country

Exogenous variables

$TFP_{j,r}$: productivity; $TFP_{PDR,r} \sim N(1,\sigma_r^2)$ or $N(1,0)$

$\overline{EMS_r}$: capacity of emergency rice stocks

σ_r : standard deviation of productivity in the paddy rice sector

$EQ_{i,r,s}$: export quota of i-th good from r-th to s-th country

$PT_{j,r}$: biofuel production target

Parameters

α_r^{XFD} : share parameter of a food composite

Θ_r : scale parameter of food composite aggregate function

$\Delta_{fd,r}$: share parameter of food composite function

ε^f : elasticity of substitution for food

Ψ : parameter related to elasticity of substitution for food

$wgt_{i,r}$: export weight

Chapters 4, 5, and 6

Endogenous variables

$\tau^{pt}_{j,r}$: subsidy rate of biofuel production target

$T^{pt}_{j,r}$: subsidy of biofuel production target

ECH_r : energy composite good for household

LQH_r : liquid energy composite good for household

$EC_{j,r}$: energy composite good

$LQ_{j,r}$: liquid energy composite good

$p^{ec}_{j,r}$: price of energy composite good

$p^{lq}_{j,r}$: price of liquid fuel composite good

p^{ech}_{r} : price of energy composite good for household

p^{lqh}_{r} : price of liquid fuel for household

Parameters

$b^{EC}_{j,r}$: scale parameter of energy composite production function

$\beta^{EC\_X}_{nlq,j,r}$: share parameter of a non-liquid energy good for energy composite production function

$\beta^{EC\_LQ}_{j,r}$: share parameter of a liquid energy composite for energy composite production function

$b^{LQ}_{j,r}$: scale parameter of a liquid energy composite production function

$\beta^{LQ}_{lq,j,r}$: share parameter of a liquid energy good for a liquid energy composite production function

$aec_{j,r}$: share parameter of an energy composite good for a domestic production function

α^{ECH}_{r} : share parameter of an energy composite good for a household utility function

$\beta^{ECH}_{nlq,r}$: share parameter of a non-liquid energy good for a household's energy composite production function

β^{LQHC}_{r} : share parameter of a liquid energy composite for a household's energy composite production function

b_r^{ECH} : scale parameter of a household's energy composite production function

$\beta_{lq,r}^{LQH}$: share parameter of a liquid energy good for a household's liquid energy composite production function

b_r^{LQH} : scale parameter of a household's liquid energy composite production function

σ^{lq} : elasticity of substitution of liquid energy goods

$\hbar$: parameter related to elasticity of substitution of liquid energy goods

σ^{lqh} : elasticity of substitution of liquid energy goods for household

Ξ : parameter related to elasticity of substitution of liquid energy goods for household

CHAPTER THREE

DOES AGRICULTURAL TRADE LIBERALISATION INCREASE RISKS OF SUPPLY-SIDE UNCERTAINTY?: EFFECTS OF PRODUCTIVITY SHOCKS AND EXPORT RESTRICTIONS ON WELFARE AND FOOD SUPPLY IN JAPAN

TETSUJI TANAKA AND NOBUHIRO HOSOE

Introduction

The agricultural sector in developed countries has been the central target of reform in multilateral trade negotiations led by the World Trade Organization (WTO) and bilateral free trade arrangements. Japan did not have an active role in those negotiations, although the benefits of free trade were immense as suggested by, for example, Anderson et al. (2006). The interested parties in Japan—farmers, politicians, and the Japanese Government, more specifically the Ministry of Agriculture, Forestry, and Fisheries (MAFF)—have called for protection and exceptional treatment for this sector, particularly for rice farming, every time new trade negotiations have been launched. Their arguments are twofold. One is the "multifunctionality" of the agricultural sector, which appreciates the (positive) externalities of agricultural activities such as protection of natural environments, rural scenery, culture, and so on, studied by the Science Council of Japan (2001). The other reason, discussed here, is "national food security"—concerning uncertainty in the food supply, which can be jeopardized by unforeseen supply-side shocks such as bad crops, war, and embargoes.[1] The MAFF stresses the promotion of domestic production to secure food supply, which is often subject to these risk factors, while considering importation as a secondary source, as the Basic Law on Food, Agriculture and Rural Areas (the Basic Law, hereinafter) states.

The concern about food supply sounds like a reasonable justification for protection in an age of uncertainty, considering the fact that Japan's food self-sufficiency rate is a mere 40%, measured on the basis of calories, which is a significantly lower rate than those of other major developed countries. While this low food self-sufficiency rate is a result of the outstanding comparative advantage of Japan's industrial sectors, it can make the Japanese economy susceptible to food shortages caused by the aforementioned shocks. In fact, bad weather in 1993 reduced the country's rice harvest by 26% compared with the average yield, the second worst year on record since 1926.[2] There was a soybean export embargo because of a serious crop failure in the US in 1973 and a grain export embargo in response to the USSR's invasion of Afghanistan in 1980.

National food security and Japan's agricultural policy

Excessive dependency on imports for food supply is considered a risk factor for Japan's national food security. MAFF (2006) established a contingency plan to secure food supplies for domestic consumption in emergencies. This plan was put into place to achieve national food security as defined in the Basic Law, which had been revised the year before. MAFF defined 2,000 kcal/person/day (about 20% less than usual) as the minimum calorie intake. The plan included several measures to secure the calorie intake, such as promoting domestic production, managing emergency stocks, and controlling food markets. Among the crops, rice has been the most important commodity for Japan. In 2004, rice comprised 23% of the population's total calorie intake, followed by wheat, which contributed 13% of the total. The government keeps large emergency stocks of rice and other major crops to secure the food supply, while making continuing efforts to increase the country's food self-sufficiency rate.

---

[1] The focus of Japan's national food security is slightly different from that of the popular concept of food security. The former is set on food security in contingency in the developed economy of Japan, the latter on food security in developing economies, which are vulnerable to shocks because of their continuing poverty in the short run and poor capability of feeding rapidly growing populations in the long run. Hayami (2000) discussed their difference in detail.

[2] The worst decline of 33% occurred in 1945.

High trade barriers on rice have played an important role in the achievement of an almost 100% of self-sufficiency rate for rice. Proponents of these trade barriers argue that they are necessary to maintain the overall self-sufficiency rate of food because the supply of other foods depends heavily on imports. Even though trade theories imply gains from trade, proposals for free rice trade have never been accepted in Japan because free trade lowers the food self-sufficiency rate, and thereby increases the dependency of the food supply on imports, which is supposed to make the food supply less secure.

The impact of agricultural trade liberalisation is twofold: (1) deterministic gains from trade achieved through the removal of trade barriers and (2) stochastic gains and losses caused by productivity shocks, whose magnitude can be exacerbated or mitigated depending on the level of trade openness. Researchers have often analysed the first aspect of trade liberalisation but have rarely examined the second aspect. This lack of analysis of the second aspect leads to people being uninformed and triggers their opposition to trade liberalisation, simply because trade liberalisation is generally believed to make the domestic economy susceptible to shocks from abroad.

The rice trade and its barriers

Japan has previously strictly prohibited imports of rice but permitted minimum access (MA) imports of rice in 1995 and their tariffication in 1999 as a part of the GATT Uruguay Round agreement. The imports account for only 10% of domestic production because of prohibitively high trade barriers. If these trade barriers are abolished, imports are expected to have a very high share in the total rice supply as suggested by previous studies, for example, Cramer et al. (1993) and Wailes (2005).

Japan's rice consumption is comprised mainly of mid- or short-grain rice (so-called japonica rice), rather than long-grain rice (indica rice). The former is strongly preferred in East Asian countries while the latter type is popular elsewhere in Asia and in other regions. Japan's rice trade patterns reflect this preference. Japan's three major rice trade partners (China, the US, and Australia) produce japonica rice and expect to increase their exports to Japan after the rice trade is liberalised.

As rice in many countries is mainly produced and consumed domestically, its international trade is thin. Only a small fraction of production is exported and imported internationally unlike wheat, maize, and so on. The top 10 rice producing countries, many of which are in Asia, cover almost 90% of the world's total production of rice. Their production fluctuates with weather conditions, including droughts, cool summer days, and cyclones/typhoons. While productivity has an upward-sloping trend, it sometimes shows sudden drops (see Figure 3.1).

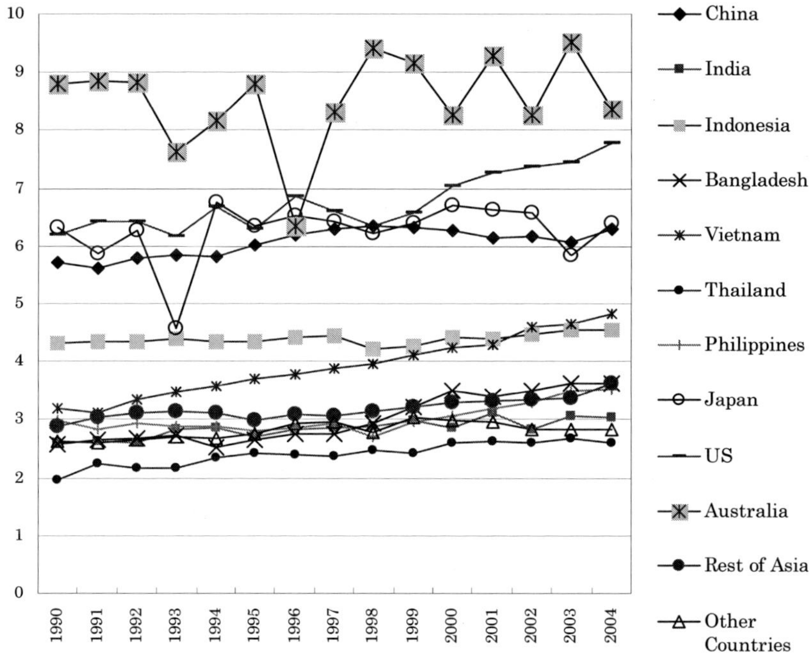

Figure 3.1: Productivity fluctuations of paddy rice [Unit: tons/hectare]
Data source: FAOSTAT

Once Japan's rice market is liberalised, any shocks in the domestic and foreign markets will directly affect its food supply. Furthermore, taking into account Japan's strong preference towards japonica rice, the international market seems much less reliable as an alternative supply source. Therefore, it might seem a reasonable idea that national food security can only be established by protecting the domestic rice market in order to maintain the self-sufficiency rate of food, rather than by depending on foreign supply sources.

Literature review

The majority of existing studies on Japan's rice trade liberalisation have been conducted from a deterministic viewpoint. Cramer et al. (1999) developed a 22-country world rice trade model and found that Japan would import three million tons of rice (about one-third of domestic consumption) with an 8% annual tariff reduction after tariffication. In their conclusion, they suggested that food security could be improved by increasing accessibility to international markets, rather than through protection. However, they did not explicitly consider whether the international markets could be reliable, considering fluctuating productivity inside and outside of Japan.

Using a spatial equilibrium model, Cramer et al. (1993) found that the removal of direct and indirect rice trade barriers in all countries would lead to increases in Japan's rice imports by about five million tons. Wailes (2005) conducted a similar but updated analysis on the elimination of tariffs and export subsidies and found that the increase in rice imports would be about two million tons. Overall, these results indicate that free rice trade would lead to imports into Japan constituting as much as 20–50% of domestic consumption. Through these imports, foreign-made shocks would affect the Japanese economy.

On the other hand, there are only a few studies that have examined agricultural trade liberalisation from the view of national food security. Hosoe (2004) developed a world trade computable general equilibrium (CGE) model to evaluate the impact of Japan's domestic productivity shock in 1993 on its own economy under rice price controls and the impact of Japan's emergency rice imports on other countries. The productivity shock was assumed to be deterministic in the sense that its magnitude was calibrated to reproduce that historical event in 1993. Most recently, Maeda and Kano (2008) examined the effect of an international rice reserve system to stabilise rice markets, using a spatial equilibrium model that considered fluctuating rice supplies using a Monte Carlo simulation method.

In this study, we ask whether it is reasonable to sacrifice gains from trade for the sake of national food security, to what extent rice supply can be secured by its stockpile, and whether Japan, as one of the world's largest economic powers, is likely to suffer from food shortages as discussed by Hayami (2000). To this end, we develop a world trade CGE model in combination with a Monte Carlo simulation method that provides a comprehensive framework to analyse international rice markets under uncertainty. We take into account risk factors such as low food self-sufficiency induced by trade liberalisation, and a wide range of productivity shocks inside and outside of Japan. This technique is similar to that used by Harris and Robinson (2001) to analyse the impact of weather fluctuations induced by El Niño on regional agricultural output and income distribution in Mexico. We also evaluate the effectiveness of the Japanese government's emergency stocks, held in preparation for a crop failure. Moreover, we simulate rice export quotas set by major rice exporters to Japan. By using a CGE model, we can depict how these shocks breaking out in the rice sector affects the macroeconomy and how rice is substituted with other foods to mitigate the impact of the shock.

This chapter proceeds as follows. We explain our world trade CGE model in Section 2 and simulation scenarios in Section 3. Simulation results are presented in Section 4. Our conclusions are provided in Section 5. In the appendix of this chapter we further report the relevant sensitivity analyses.

Structure of the world trade CGE model

While using the basic structure of the single-country CGE model described by Devarajan et al. (1990), we extend the model to create a multicountry model to analyse international rice markets under uncertainty. Reflecting the fact that Japan's rice trading partners are mostly Asia-Pacific countries, we distinguish 12 regions using the Global Trade Analysis Project (GTAP) database (version 7.1).[3] Each region has eight sectors, including five food-related sectors (Table 3.1). Each sector is represented by a perfectly competitive profit-maximizing firm with a Leontief production function for gross output and with a constant elasticity of substitution (CES) production function for value-added components (Figure 2.3). For the elasticity of substitution, we assume 0.2 for the agricultural sectors (paddy rice, wheat, and other agriculture) and 1.0 for the other sectors.[4] Among the value-added components, capital is assumed to be immobile among sectors in order to model relatively short-run phenomena under unforeseen shocks in all simulations (except Scenario M, discussed later) presuming a situation where productivity shocks are observed after allocation of capital has been determined.[5] In contrast,

---

[3] For more information about the GTAP database, see Hertel (1997).

[4] Even when we alternatively assume 0.1 or 1.0 for this elasticity in these agricultural sectors, our conclusions are found to be almost qualitatively robust. Details are shown in the appendix.

[5] When we alternatively assume all the factors are mobile, Japan and other countries can absorb such shocks more flexibly and experience smaller welfare fluctuations. This alternative assumption reinforces rather than undermines the robustness of our conclusions.

labour is assumed to be mobile among sectors. International factor mobility is not assumed. These factors are assumed to be fully employed with flexible factor price adjustments.

Table 3.1: List of regions and sectors in the model

Region	Sector
Japan	Paddy rice*
China	Wheat*
India	Other agriculture*
Indonesia	Processed rice*
Bangladesh	Other food*
Vietnam	Manufacturing
Thailand	Services
Philippines	Transportation
US	
Australia	
Rest of Asia	
Other countries	

Note: Asterisks indicate food commodities used for the food composite.

Sectoral gross outputs are split into domestic outputs and composite exports using a constant elasticity of transformation (CET) function. The domestic goods and composite imports are aggregated into composite goods using a CES function as assumed by Armington (1969). The composite imports consist of imports from various regions, and the composite exports are decomposed into exports to various regions. For these CES/CET functions, we use the elasticity of substitution as suggested in the GTAP database. The elasticity of substitution represents the similarity of goods differentiated by the origin and destination of trade. For example, the elasticity of substitution between the domestic goods and the composite imports is assumed to be 5.05 for paddy rice and 2.60 for processed rice.[6] With this nested CES structure, we can describe how rice trade liberalisation lowers import prices leading to the substitution of domestic production by foreign rice. We can also describe how shocks inside and outside Japan are propagated through the international rice trade.

[6] We assume no active stock behaviour except in the case considering Japan's emergency stocks in scenario S, discussed later.

Although we do not explicitly control for the different types of rice grains in our model, the nested CES structure approximately reflects Japan's preference for japonica rice. Share parameters in the CES functions are calibrated in order to reproduce the actual trade flows of rice, mainly from countries that produce japonica rice. Exchange rates are flexibly adjusted so that the current account balance remains constant in US dollar terms in all regions.

Composite goods are used for consumption by the household, as well as for government, investment, and intermediate input.[7] If the commodity is one of the food commodities listed in Table 3.1, it is aggregated into a food composite along with other food commodities. The food composite contributes to utility (Figure 2.4). This structure describes substitution among foods in household consumption with a CES function, which gives flexibility to our assumptions about the price elasticity of food consumption demand. Surveying existing literature, we assume that its elasticity of substitution is 0.1.[8] If the commodity is not a food, it contributes directly to utility.[9]

Simulation scenarios

To quantify the welfare impact of Japan's rice trade liberalisation on the country's national food security, we conduct comparative static analyses considering the following scenario factors: (1) unilateral abolition of trade barriers on paddy and processed rice imports by Japan; (2) fluctuations of productivity in the paddy rice sector; (3) emergency stocks to mitigate the adverse impact of anticipated productivity shocks; and (4) quotas on rice exports imposed by the four major rice exporters to Japan. We set up 11 scenarios to determine the extent to which Japan's national food security is jeopardized or ensured by these scenario factors identified in Table 3.2.

---

[7] See footnote 6.

[8] Generally, the price elasticity of necessities like rice is supposed to be very small. However, there is a variety of rice price elasticity estimates ranging from zero or 0.1 to 2.8. A survey of these parameter estimates and a sensitivity analysis with respect to this elasticity are provided in the appendix. Our simulation results are also found to be qualitatively robust in this sensitivity analysis.

[9] The complete list of model equations is provided in the annex.

Table 3.2: Scenario design

Scenario	Trade libera-lization	Shocks in		Rice stocks	Capital mobility	Export quotas
		Japan	Rest of the world			
T0	–	–	–	–	–	–
T1	x	–	–	–	–	–
R0	–	–	x	–	–	–
R1	x	–	x	–	–	–
J0	–	x	–	–	–	–
J1	x	x	–	–	–	–
A0	–	x	x	–	–	–
A1	x	x	x	–	–	–
S	–	x	x	x	–	–
M	x	–	–	–	x	–
Q	x	–	–	–	–	x

The first two scenarios, T0 and T1, are conventional ones used to assess deterministic gains from trade. As no shock is assumed in Scenario T0 as a base run, its results are nothing but the original GTAP data. The six subsequent scenarios are used to investigate the impact of trade liberalisation on regimes subject to productivity shocks in Japan (Scenarios J0 and J1), the rest of the world (Scenarios R0 and R1), and all over the world (Scenarios A0 and A1). Scenario S is used to analyse the effectiveness of the government stocks. The last two Scenarios M and Q are used to evaluate the impact of possible export quota impositions by rice exporters. Details of those scenario factors are provided below.

Scenario factor 1: Abolition of trade barriers

We assume unilateral abolition of tariff and nontariff barriers by Japan which are reported by the GTAP database. The tariff rates and tariff-equivalent trade barriers on paddy and processed rice imports generally reach several hundred percent. Neither border barriers in the other sectors nor those in the other regions are changed.

Scenario factor 2: Productivity shocks

We assume that productivity shocks happen randomly to the total factor productivity parameter of the gross output production function in the paddy rice sector, following the independent identically distributed normal distribution $N(1,\sigma_r^2)$ for region r. We measure the productivity of the paddy rice sector by production per acre of harvested area and estimate the standard deviations σ_r of the productivity of these 12 regions with time series data for 15 years (1990–2004) provided by FAOSTAT, while removing the effect of the time trend on productivity (Table 3.3).[1] We simulate 1,000 Monte Carlo draws for each scenario. Among our 1,000 draws, Australia shows the worst maximum productivity decline (26% compared with the mean yield) among the 12 regions, followed by Japan. In the other regions, maximum productivity declines are about 10–20%.

When an adverse productivity shock takes place in Japan—whose domestic output is almost only for domestic use—the country's domestic consumption is reduced but is supported partly by imported rice. Similarly, when an abundant rice crop is harvested in Japan, the surplus can be absorbed abroad. Under a freer rice trade regime, Japan can access international rice markets more easily and manage shocks to its domestic production through imports more flexibly. In view of the statistical distribution of domestic welfare, given the same magnitude of productivity shocks, trade liberalisation itself shifts the mean of the welfare distribution upwards and decreases the standard deviation of the welfare distribution (the upper graph of Figure 3.2). In this case, whether a productivity shock is negative or positive, trade liberalisation always brings about a preferable impact on welfare distribution.

In contrast to these cases with productivity shocks in Japan, when an adverse productivity shock takes place in the rest of the world, particularly in China, the US, or Australia, Japan's imports from these countries are jeopardized. As protectionists warn, rice trade liberalisation increases Japan's dependency on imported food and thus can exacerbate the impact of adverse productivity shocks on Japan. However, if a positive productivity shock takes place in those countries, Japan can conversely gain by the same mechanism. As the productivity parameter, by definition, is distributed around its mean, such productivity shocks as a whole do not seriously deteriorate the mean of the welfare distribution in Japan. Instead, they increase the standard deviation of the welfare distribution while trade liberalisation brings deterministic gains through improvements of efficiency in resource allocation (the lower graph of Figure 3.2). In this

[1] The estimated residuals do not seem spatially correlated by simple examination using a correlation matrix. Even if we assume a doubling of the standard deviations for productivity in all the regions for our simulations, we find our conclusions qualitatively robust in general. Results are summarized in the appendix and the annex.

case, without combining the impact of trade liberalisation with those of productivity shocks on the distribution of welfare, we cannot judge immediately whether trade liberalisation is always welfare improving.

Table 3.3: Regression results of paddy rice productivity [Dependent variable: rice productivity index (2001=1.00)]

	Regression results of paddy rice productivity				Monte Carlo draws	
	Intercept	Time trend	SD of residuals	R^2	Min.	Max.
Japan	–9.7352 (–1.02)	0.0053 (1.12)	0.0801	0.088	0.75	1.31
China	–12.9460 (–4.16)**	0.0070 (4.47)**	0.0261	0.606	0.91	1.08
India	–15.6576 (–3.1)**	0.0083 (3.28)**	0.0423	0.453	0.87	1.16
Indonesia	–4.2802 (–1.93)*	0.0026 (2.38)**	0.0186	0.304	0.94	1.07
Bangladesh	–47.7156 (–8.57)**	0.0243 (8.73)**	0.0467	0.854	0.84	1.13
Vietnam	–54.6946 (–28.85)**	0.0278 (29.33)**	0.0159	0.985	0.95	1.05
Thailand	–35.8382 (–10.17)**	0.0184 (10.43)**	0.0295	0.893	0.89	1.10
Philippines	–22.8654 (–3.82)**	0.0119 (3.97)**	0.0502	0.548	0.83	1.16
US	–26.4873 (–6.07)**	0.0137 (6.28)**	0.0366	0.752	0.86	1.11
Australia	–5.9156 (–0.56)	0.0034 (0.65)	0.0885	0.031	0.74	1.25
Rest of Asia	–19.6074 (–7.76)**	0.0103 (8.14)**	0.0212	0.836	0.94	1.07
Other countries	–33.3938 (–12.26)**	0.0172 (12.6)**	0.0228	0.924	0.93	1.08

Note: T-values are in parentheses. * and ** indicate parameters are significant at 10% and 5% significance levels, respectively.

Means (=1.00) and standard deviations (SD) of the Monte Carlo draws are all consistent with those of the original estimates for the residuals.

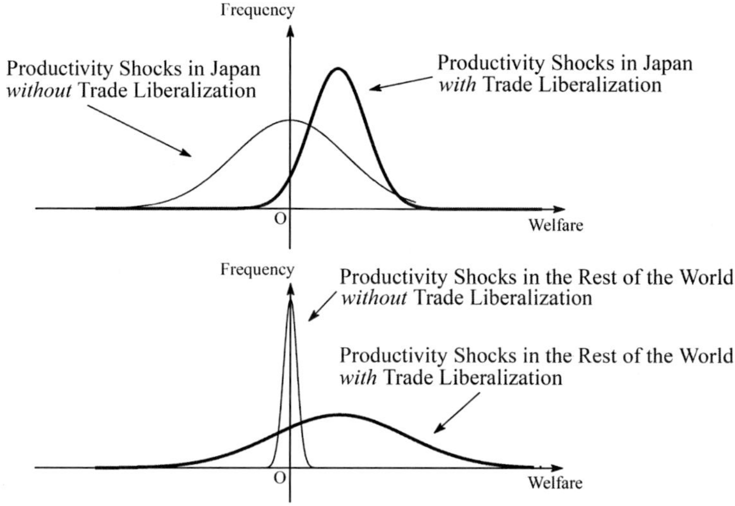

Figure 3.2: Impact of productivity shocks and trade liberalisation on distribution of Japan's welfare

Scenario factor 3: Emergency stocks

Preparing emergency stocks is a popular measure used for coping with bad crops. The impact of the rice supply shock in 1993 was exacerbated partly by the government-led restructuring of Japan's food system. The government had significantly reduced its rice stocks to 0.23 million tons, covering 2.5% of consumption in a normal year. After the bad harvest in 1993, the government increased the size of the emergency stocks to 1.5 million tons, equivalent to 17% of the annual production in 2004. We assume this stock is held and is released only when a negative productivity shock takes place in Japan, so as to maintain the original domestic paddy rice supply. When the losses of paddy rice production exceed the size of the emergency stocks prepared in advance, the market mechanism starts to work with a flexible price adjustment and imports begin to increase. The emergency stocks truncate a part of the lower shoulder of the distribution of the rice supply (Figure 3.3). Among the 1,000 draws, 493 cases are expected to bring about negative productivity shocks in Japan. The emergency stocks are found to be large enough to fully cover the lost rice yield in 95% of those negative productivity cases.

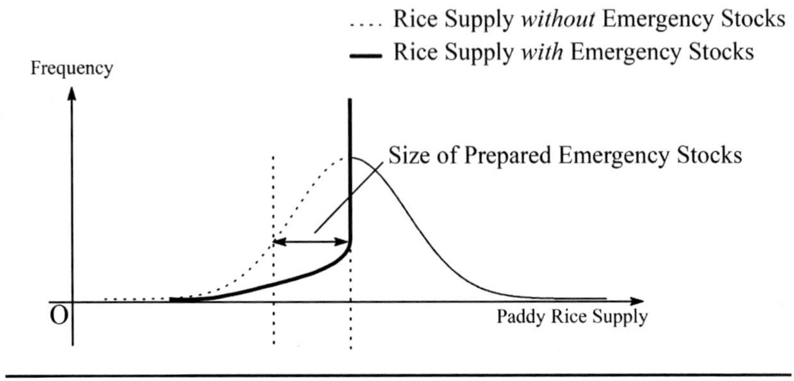

Figure 3.3: Distribution of rice supply and effects of emergency stocks

To simplify our comparative statics, we assume that the emergency stocks are prepared before a shock occurs and that the release of the emergency stocks does not bring any special capital gains or losses to the government. By comparing the simulation results of Scenario A0 with those of Scenario S, we can quantify the benefits of the emergency stocks measured with a welfare indicator. In addition, by subtracting the storage costs of the emergency stocks from the benefits, we can see the net benefits of the emergency stocks.

Scenario factor 4: Export quotas

While productivity shocks jeopardize both the domestic and the foreign rice supply every year, export quotas damage Japan by limiting the foreign supply. In designing scenarios for the quota analysis, we need some reconsideration of the reference equilibrium, which describes the status quo. If we simulate export quotas based simply on the reference equilibrium that is characterized by the abundant domestic rice production capacity and the very low penetration of foreign rice (i.e., Scenario T0), it is obvious that the impact of quota imposition should be negligibly small. We cannot derive any significant implications from such a simulation analysis.

In reality, the damage from export quotas is serious when Japan has substituted imported rice for domestic rice under the free rice trade regime and has reduced its domestic production capacity by reallocating factors (particularly capital) away from the paddy rice sector in the long run. Especially for this quota analysis, this situation is computed by assuming rice trade liberalisation with inter-sectoral mobility of all the factors and defining a new reference equilibrium—let it be referred to as the intermediate equilibrium (Scenario M). Then, we assume no inter-sectoral mobility of capital and simulate export quotas set by the four major rice exporters, Australia, China, Thailand, and the US, to Japan (Scenario Q). The size of the export quota is assumed to be as large as the original import level from these exporters described in Scenario T0.

Simulation results

We simulate random productivity shocks and various policies and quantify the costs and benefits of trade liberalisation for the Japanese economy. The simulation results are summarized in Table 3.4 and presented graphically in Figure 3.4.

Table 3.4: Summary statistics of simulation results for Japan

Scenario	Welfare (EV)					Import price of processed rice		Calorie intake	Self-suff. rate of rice
	Min.	Mean	Max.	SD	% of GDP	Mean	SD	Min.	Mean
		[mil. US$]			Mean/GDP	[base=1.00]		[kcal/person /day]	[%]
T0	–	0	–	–	0.00	1.00	–	2,564	94.2
T1	–	4,453	–	–	0.10	0.28	–	2,622	62.4
R0	–102	0	94	26	0.00	1.01	0.04	2,562	94.2
R1	4,202	4,454	4,710	69	0.10	0.28	0.01	2,619	62.4
J0	–8,358	–319	3,515	1609	-0.01	1.00	0.01	2,474	93.7
J1	1,561	4,371	6,589	707	0.10	0.28	0.00	2,602	62.1
A0	–8,216	–319	3,518	1609	-0.01	1.01	0.04	2,476	93.7
A1	1,711	4,371	6,558	710	0.10	0.28	0.01	2,603	62.1
S	–6,019	–57	3,518	1229	0.00	1.00	0.02	2,521	91.5
M	–	5,707	–	–	0.13	0.29	–	2,611	36.0
Q	–	–15,340	–	–	-0.34	1.20	–	2,334	46.8

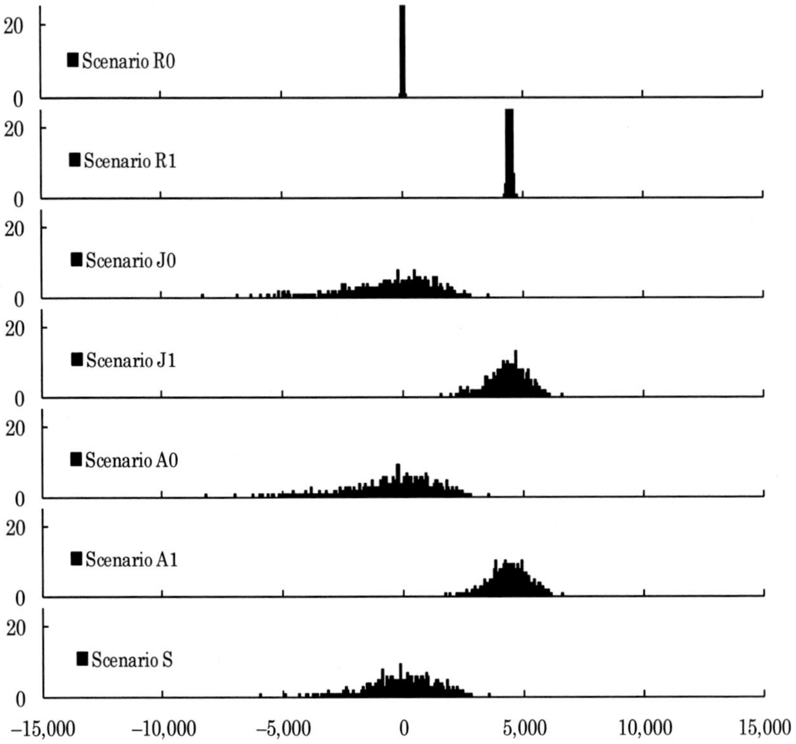

Figure 3.4: Distribution of Japan's welfare [Unit: EV in millions of US dollars]

Deterministic impact of trade liberalisation

When we assume abolition of all the tariff and nontariff barriers on paddy and processed rice imports by Japan (Scenario T1), imports of paddy and processed rice surge to reduce Japan's paddy rice production by 30% compared with Scenario T0.[2] Rice consumption is increased by 8%

[2] The increase of japonica rice imports by Japan has to be consistent with export capacity of the four major rice exporters, particularly China, where japonica rice is not produced in large quantities. We do not distinguish among the various rice types in our model or consider exporters' supply capacities of japonica rice, but approximate Japan's preference toward japonica rice and exporters' japonica rice supply capacity with the nested CES/CET structure. Thus, it is difficult to examine the validity of our model and results directly. In this regard, the simulation results

because of consumers exploiting the falls in rice prices. As a result, the overall welfare gains measured by equivalent variations (EV) are US$4,453 million.

Productivity shocks in the rest of the world

People are often concerned that when they are heavily dependent on foreign supply sources for rice, the food supply could be insecure because of unforeseen productivity shocks in other countries. A comparison of results between Scenarios R0 and R1 indicates whether these concerns are reasonable or just imaginary. The results of Scenario R0 show no change from those of Scenario T0 in the mean of Japan's welfare distribution, but do show some change in its volatility. [3] The welfare distribution of Scenario R0 (and Scenarios J0 and A0, discussed later) indicates that without liberalising rice imports there is no statistically significant chance for Japan to attain the deterministic gain achieved in Scenario T1.

Abolition of trade barriers on rice imports increases the penetration of foreign rice, which is subject to productivity shocks. The results of Scenario R1 show that trade liberalisation increases both the mean and the standard deviation of welfare compared with those of Scenario R0. This increase in volatility is, however, not so large that it brings a case for Japan to suffer negative welfare impact among the 1,000 cases. Furthermore, the worst welfare level (US$4,202 million) achieved under free rice trade (Scenario R1) is far better than the best welfare level (US$94 million) without free rice trade (Scenario R0).

The impact of productivity shocks in foreign countries can be confirmed by examining import prices for Japan. While rice trade liberalisation lowers the import price of processed rice by about 70% on average, its price fluctuations seem to be almost nil. Therefore, the productivity shocks abroad do not cause any price hikes or adversely affect household rice consumption.

---

of other studies where several rice types were distinguished may help us to estimate China's export supply capacity of japonica rice. For example, Cramer et al. (1993) predicted that trade liberalization would cause China to significantly increase exports of both indica and japonica rice by 6–7 million tons in total, where japonica would comprise about 35–40% of its total exports. A similar finding was reported by Wailes (2005).

[3] The mean of the welfare impact is found to be slightly negative in scenarios J0 and A0, where we assume only productivity shocks. This is because of the concavity of the utility function, which implies risk-averseness of preferences represented by the nested CES utility function.

Productivity shocks in Japan

When we simulate productivity shocks in Japan, the value of trade liberalisation during productivity shocks can be assessed from a different viewpoint. The simulation results of Scenario J0 show that domestic productivity shocks without trade liberalisation would bring about significantly large volatilities in welfare. This is because the domestic market is isolated from alternative supply sources abroad because of high trade barriers.

With productivity shocks in Japan, trade liberalisation brings the country a double dividend (Scenario J1)—a higher welfare mean and a lower welfare volatility. By integrating the domestic market with foreign rice markets, Japan can pool the risk of productivity shocks internationally.

Impact of productivity shocks all over the world

Comparing the simulation results of Scenarios R0, R1, J0, and J1, we found that the domestic productivity shocks are the dominant factor in determining the mean and the volatility of Japan's welfare distribution. Thus, when we assume random productivity shocks all over the world, with and without trade liberalisation, the simulation results of Scenarios A0 and A1 are similar to those of Scenarios J0 and J1, respectively. These results do not support the idea that trade liberalisation—even with the uncertainty of productivity shocks—is a risky policy for the Japanese economy, either.

While we have described the distributions of welfare, we can also obtain distributions for consumption of rice and other foods, which indicates levels of calorie intake. None of these simulation results indicates any serious food shortages (i.e., calorie intake lower than 2,000 kcal/person/day).

Effectiveness of emergency stocks

Releasing the emergency stocks in bad crop situations in Scenario S, the upper tail of the price distribution becomes thinner (Figure 3.5). The highest price of processed rice is 1.33 in Scenario S, while it is 1.72 in Scenario A0. The release of stocks seems to succeed in stabilising the domestic market and securing the rice supply. However, the welfare impact is not so remarkable. The emergency stocks increase the mean welfare by US$262 million, compared with the result of Scenario A0. Overall, the volatility of welfare does not decrease markedly.

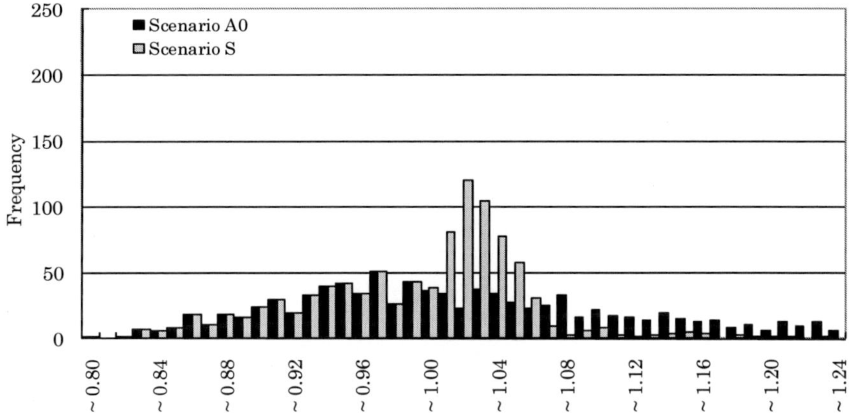

Figure 3.5: Effects of emergency stocks on the domestic processed rice price in Japan. [Unit: Price index calibrated to the base run price (=1.00)]

While the larger stocks can make the food supply more secure, maintaining those stocks becomes more costly. We have to assess the extent to which the emergency stocks can stabilise the domestic market against productivity fluctuations and achieve better national welfare. MAFF (2001) reported that the annual storage costs of the emergency stocks in Japan reached ten thousand yen per ton (US$178 million in total).[4] In addition to the storage costs, the rice stock depreciates during storage. Its capital losses amount to US$253 million per annum.[5] Given these facts, it does not seem that emergency stocks are worth maintaining when we assume risk-neutral or moderately risk-averse people. This result suggests that we should reduce the amount of emergency stocks or store them somewhere abroad, where cheaper storage costs are offered. For example, the International Crop Reserve Research Workshop (2001) reported annual storage costs to be US$22.5 per ton of paddy rice in Thailand. In this case, the annual storage costs of 1.5 million tons of brown rice amount to US$42 million. Although the risk would have to be accommodated during transportation between the distant warehouses and Japan, the expected net benefits of stocking rice abroad would be

[4] Using the average exchange rate of 118.59 yen per US dollar.

[5] In this rough estimate, the depreciation rate and the unit price of government rice stocks are assumed to be 10% and 0.2 yen per ton, respectively. Regarding the depreciation rate, Rice Stable Supply Support Organization (2007) reported a 6–19% decline in sales prices of the government stocks in a crop year.

positive.[6]

Impact of export quotas

If we consider the full inter-sectoral reallocation of factors induced by rice trade liberalisation in Japan, we find a more drastic contraction of the domestic paddy rice sector by 60% and larger foreign rice penetration (Scenario M). After computing this intermediate equilibrium, we again assume inter-sectoral immobility of capital and simulate export quota imposition (Scenario Q). (No productivity shocks are assumed here, because the previous simulation results show that they do not significantly jeopardize the Japanese economy under a free rice trade regime.) Japan suffers far larger welfare deterioration of US$15,340 million from the quota imposition than the gains of US$5,707 million from free trade in a normal year computed in Scenario M, as well as lower calorie intake of 2,334 kcal/person/day.[7]

A rice shortage caused by quotas by the four exporters could be mitigated by increasing imports from other regions and/or by substituting rice with other foods. However, the former measure requires a large increase of imports and causes a price increase; the latter is not easy since we assume a small elasticity of food substitution. Moreover, in this scenario it is difficult for domestic production to respond to the rice shortage, partly because a large amount of capital has been reallocated away from the rice sectors and partly because labour, the only mobile factor in Scenario Q, cannot flexibly substitute for the lost capital due to the assumed small elasticity of substitution between factors. This is suggested by the results of the sensitivity analysis shown in the appendix. The adverse impact of quota imposition is found to be smaller in cases with larger elasticity of substitution among foods or between factors.

We should consider two points in interpreting these results. One is that

---

[6] The robustness of our conclusion in this regard is examined under various assumptions in our CGE model. Among several alternative cases, the benefits of the stock significantly exceed its costs (including depreciation of the rice stock) only in a few cases when we assume the stock is held in Thailand. One is the case with a small elasticity of substitution (=0.1) in the CES function for value added in the agricultural sectors. The other is the case with a doubled value of the standard deviation of the productivity shocks in all the regions. Details are shown in the appendix.

[7] As the intermediate equilibrium computed by scenario M is defined as a new reference, we should compare results of scenario Q with those of scenario M while their results are expressed in terms of changes from the base run (i.e., scenario T0).

while we have conducted a Monte Carlo simulation with respect to the productivity shock in the previous simulations, we introduce the export quotas in a deterministic manner in this particular simulation. That is, the welfare impact of Scenario Q suggests only a conditional welfare impact given the imposition of export quotas. Depending on the assumption about the probability that export quotas are set by the four countries, our overall evaluation differs. If we expect such an emergency situation to take place frequently, say, once every three or four years, the overall net benefit of rice trade liberalisation would be negative. In contrast, if the emergency situation were to happen as seldom as once every 10 or 100 years, we may well expect the adverse impact of the export quota to be much smaller than the gains attained in usual situations without the export quota.

Historically speaking, Japan has experienced an effective embargo only once, during World War II. Although a brief embargo-like situation occurred in 1973, when the US halved its soybean exports for two months, it was surprising that at that time Japan increased crop imports despite a sharp price rise, as Hayami (2000) pointed out. In 2008, while China and some rice importers like the Philippines and Indonesia banned or restricted rice exports in reaction to skyrocketing food prices from the recent commodities boom, Thailand, a large net rice exporter, stated that it would never restrict rice exports. Cambodia, another net rice exporter, had set a ban on its rice exports for two months at the time but resumed exporting. In addition, the US and Australia—the major rice exporters to the Japanese market—have not taken any special measures for rice to date. Three out of the four major exporters to Japan have not set any rice export restrictions since the end of World War II.

The second point is that while liberalisation of Japan's rice trade and the resulting contraction of its domestic production indicate its commitment to foreign supplies, these counterpart countries also commit their exports to Japan. Comparing the welfare impact in Scenarios M and Q, we find that Thailand, the US, and Australia would suffer from their own quota imposition while China would slightly gain (Table 3.5). For those three countries that stand to lose from imposing export quotas, it would be unreasonable to impose such quotas. Although we can only guess about the probability of them imposing export quotas, this probability would not be high considering the increasing economic interdependence of these countries within the world economy in recent years.

Table 3.5: Welfare impact in Scenarios M and Q

	(1) Scenario M	(2) Scenario Q	(2)–(1)	
	[mil. US$]	[mil. US$]	[mil. US$]	[% of GDP]
Japan	5,707	–15,340	–21,047	–0.47
China	460	474	13	0.00
India	147	781	634	0.10
Indonesia	16	28	12	0.00
Bangladesh	–2	–19	–17	–0.03
Vietnam	84	1,217	1,133	2.87
Thailand	427	51	–375	–0.23
Philippines	7	–50	–57	–0.07
US	586	–836	–1,422	–0.01
Australia	59	–131	–189	–0.03
Rest of Asia	258	2,293	2,035	0.13
Other countries	–85	–126	–41	–0.00
Total	7,664	–11,656	–19,320	–0.05

Concluding remarks

To analyse the impact of factors that can secure or endanger Japan's national food security, we developed a world trade CGE model and carried out Monte Carlo simulations. The major findings of our analysis are as follows. First, if rice productivity shocks are anticipated abroad, there is no statistically significant chance for the Japanese economy to be worse off under freer rice trade. Second, in the case of domestic productivity shocks, rice trade liberalisation not only increases the welfare mean but also decreases its volatility. Combining these two findings, protection of the domestic rice market harms, rather than ensures, Japan's national food security. MAFF's policy of pursuing higher food self-sufficiency through protectionist policies for rice is thus nonsensical. Freer rice trade should be accepted with some side payments to compensate farmers for their losses by an influx of foreign rice. Moreover, the criterion of ensuring the minimum calorie intake of 2,000 kcal/person/day also has no significance because Japan would never suffer such poor nutrition from any realistic productivity shocks. Third, the emergency stock is not cost effective. The stock should be reduced or kept in other countries that offer cheaper storage. Finally, if export quotas were set by the four major rice exporters to Japan, Japan would suffer considerably. However, three of these nations are unlikely to impose such quotas because they would also suffer from such quotas. As discussed above, even if we take into account the concerns of the protectionists, national food security is found to be a very poor rationale for agricultural protection.

Some reservations regarding our analysis should be mentioned. Households are often very sensitive to a slight shortfall in essential commodities like food, but do not benefit much from a good harvest once they are satisfied with their level of food consumption, particularly in developed countries. Because the border barriers reported in the GTAP database are estimated on the basis of gaps between domestic and international prices, they tend to be overestimated. Thus, the actual foreign rice penetration and, thus, gains from trade might be smaller than our estimates. We can verify our simulation results by assuming lower original protection levels and functional forms for the household utility function.

While we focus only on the official emergency stocks in Japan, we ignore rice inventories held by private agents like dealers and active stock management by exporters in reaction to their own domestic prices. We would find the effectiveness of the official emergency stocks to be much smaller and the risk of food shortages lower if we consider these stocks as well.

Appendix: Sensitivity analysis

We have conducted sensitivity analyses with respect to three key parameters of our CGE model (Table A3.1) as well as the volatility of productivity shocks. They are as follows.

Table A3.1: Assumed key elasticity and its alternative values used in sensitivity analysis

Sector	Elasticity of substitution		
	Armington composite	Food composite	Value added
Paddy rice	5.05#		0.2*
Wheat	4.45		0.2*
Other agriculture	2.23	0.1	0.2*
Processed rice	2.60#		1.0
Other food	2.48		1.0
Manufacturing	3.56	–	1.0
Services	1.94	–	1.0
Transportation	1.90	–	1.0
Sensitivity analysis	**Alternative elasticity**		
	+30%, –30% for the rice sectors (#)	1.0	0.1, 1.0 for the agricultural sectors (*)

Source: Elasticity of substitution for the Armington composite: the GTAP database version 7.1.

Sensitivity analysis: Armington elasticity

Elasticity of substitution for the Armington aggregation $1/(1-\eta_i)$ and elasticity of transformation for gross output $1/(\phi_i-1)$ are obtained from the GTAP database (Table A3.1). These elasticities are doubled for the elasticity for import variety aggregation $1/(1-\varpi_i)$ and for export variety production $1/(\varphi_i-1)$. We carried out sensitivity analyses of our simulation results with respect to the Armington elasticity of substitution for the paddy rice and the processed rice sectors. We alternatively assumed 30% larger and smaller elasticities for the paddy rice and the processed rice sectors, respectively. The results are reported in Tables A3.2–A3.3. In cases of smaller elasticity, the deterministic gains from trade become relatively smaller. Consequently, the two distributions of welfare, with and without rice trade liberalisation, get slightly closer to overlapping with each other in Scenarios J0, J1, A0, and A1. The emergency stocks (kept in Japan) are not found to be cost-effective, either. Smaller elasticity tends to generate smaller import penetration and thus smaller gains from trade in Scenario M and smaller damage from quota imposition in Scenario Q.

Table A3.2: Summary statistics of simulation results for Japan (with elasticity of substitution: –30 %)

	Welfare (EV)					Import price of processed rice		Calorie intake	Self-suff. rate of rice
Scenario	Min.	Mean	Max.	SD	% of GDP	Mean	SD	Min.	Mean
		[mil. US$]			Mean/GDP	[base=1.00]		[kcal/person /day]	[%]
T0	–	0	–	–	0.00	1.00	–	2,564	94.2
T1	–	3,323	–	–	0.07	0.29	–	2,608	76.2
R0	–95	–0	89	24	0.00	1.01	0.04	2,563	94.2
R1	3,164	3,323	3,464	41	0.07	0.29	0.01	2,606	76.2
J0	–9,716	–358	3,506	1695	-0.01	1.00	0.01	2,445	93.8
J1	–1,003	3,187	5,874	937	0.07	0.29	0.00	2,569	75.9
A0	–9,636	–358	3,508	1695	-0.01	1.01	0.05	2,447	93.8
A1	–895	3,187	5,863	938	0.07	0.29	0.01	2,571	76.0
S	–6,477	–62	3,508	1243	0.00	1.00	0.02	2,513	91.4
M	–	3,280	–	–	0.07	0.31	–	2,591	68.5
Q	–	–4,484	–	–	-0.10	1.12	–	2,475	81.3

Table A3.3: Summary statistics of simulation results for Japan (with elasticity of substitution: +30 %)

	Welfare (EV)					Import price of processed rice		Calorie intake	Self-suff. rate of rice
Scenario	Min.	Mean	Max.	SD	% of GDP	Mean	SD	Min.	Mean
		[mil. US$]			Mean/GDP	[base=1.00]		[kcal/person /day]	[%]
T0	–	0	–	–	0.00	1.00	–	2,564	94.2
T1	–	5,493	–	–	0.12	0.27	–	2,632	44.8
R0	–109	0	100	28	0.00	1.01	0.04	2,562	94.2
R1	5,137	5,494	5,880	103	0.12	0.28	0.01	2,629	44.7
J0	–7,450	–286	3,508	1538	-0.01	1.00	0.01	2,492	93.5
J1	3,385	5,439	7,251	546	0.12	0.28	0.01	2,618	44.4
A0	–7,255	–285	3,512	1537	-0.01	1.01	0.04	2,495	93.5
A1	3,574	5,440	7,193	556	0.12	0.28	0.01	2,620	44.4
S	–5,635	–54	3,512	1212	0.00	1.00	0.02	2,527	91.5
M	–	9,594	–	–	0.21	0.27	–	2,643	5.5
Q	–	–22,047	–	–	-0.49	1.12	–	2,246	7.5

Sensitivity analysis: Price elasticity of food consumption

We use 0.1 for the elasticity of substitution ε^f in the food composite CES function, which is approximately equal to the price elasticity of food consumption demand. However, this elasticity might be too small considering the fact that there are a variety of estimates for the price elasticity of rice demand in Japan (Table A3.4). As the majority of recent estimates suggest that the elasticity is smaller than unity but these estimates have never converged to any conclusive magnitude to date, we conduct a sensitivity analysis with respect to this elasticity.

We alternatively assume 1.0 for ε^f. Since larger elasticity makes the household consumption more sensitive to price falls from rice trade liberalisation, the volatility of welfare is larger in the free trade Scenarios R1, J1, and A1 (Table A3.5). Nevertheless, our conclusion about the benefit of free rice trade is found to be robust. The result of our sensitivity analysis also suggests that our finding about the ineffectiveness of the emergency rice stocks demonstrated in Scenario S is robust. With larger elasticity, people can adjust to the shocks of quota imposition more flexibly. Thus, the adverse impact of quota imposition is found smaller in Scenario Q.

Table A3.4: Estimates of price elasticity of rice demand

	Estimates of price elasticity	Type of rice[/1]	Sample period	Type of sample	Data source[/2]
Otsuka (1984)	0.095–0.127	Rice	1955–80	annual	FIES; Farming Household Survey
Sawada (1984)	0.2153–0.4091 1.4161–2.7977	GMR PMR	1963–79	annual	FIES
Sawada (1985)	1.07 1.21	PMR	1972–75 1976–82	pooled	FIES
Kobayashi (1988)	0.280 0.184 0.103	GMR Rice	1968–84 1968–84 1974–84	annual annual	FIES Food Balance Sheet
Kusakari (1991)	0.469 1.104 0.919	PMR GMR Category 1, 2 GSPR	1981–88	monthly	Rice and Crop Consumption Survey; Annual Report of Rice and Crops Market Price
Hasebe (1996)	1.811 0.365	PMR GSPR	1969–73, 77–86	annual	FIES
Kako *et al.* (1997)	0.130	Rice	1970–91	annual	FIES
Chino (2000)	0.3315	Rice	1970–1994	annual	Food Balance Sheet
Chern (2001)	0.140	Rice	1986–95	pooled	FIES
Chern *et al.* (2002)	1.824 1.551–1.906	Rice (all sample) Rice (by 5 income groups)	1997	cross-section	FIES

Note: Only estimates statistically significant at conventional significance levels and with the appropriate sign are shown here.

/1 GMR: government-marketed rice, PMR: privately marketed rice, and GSPR: government standard price rice.

/2 FIES: Family Income and Expenditure Survey.

Table A3.5: Summary statistics of simulation results for Japan (ε^f =1.0)

	Welfare (EV)					Import price of processed rice		Calorie intake	Self-suff. rate of rice
Scenario	Min.	Mean	Max.	SD	% of GDP	Mean	SD	Min.	Mean
		[mil. US$]			Mean/GDP	[base=1.00]		[kcal/person /day]	[%]
T0	–	0	–	–	0.00	1.00	–	2,564	94.2
T1	–	5,970	–	–	0.13	0.31	–	2,648	57.6
R0	–73	–1	64	21	0.00	1.00	0.02	2,563	94.2
R1	5,699	5,967	6,234	78	0.13	0.31	0.00	2,644	57.6
J0	–6,346	–232	3,432	1407	-0.01	1.00	0.01	2,514	94.0
J1	2,464	5,865	8,504	862	0.13	0.31	0.00	2,618	57.3
A0	–6,340	–233	3,420	1408	-0.01	1.00	0.02	2,515	94.0
A1	2,546	5,863	8,452	865	0.13	0.31	0.01	2,619	57.3
S	–5,072	–52	3,420	1159	0.00	1.00	0.01	2,536	91.3
M	–	6,119	–	–	0.14	0.30	–	2,620	36.2
Q	–	–3,320	–	–	-0.07	0.80	–	2,504	54.9

Sensitivity analysis: Value added aggregation

While we assume 0.2 for the elasticity of substitution between primary factors in the agricultural sectors (Table A3.1), we alternatively assume 0.1 (Table A3.6) and 1.0 (Table A3.7) to be the elasticities in this sensitivity analysis. The results indicate that the less elastic assumption leads to smaller gains from trade. The net benefits of the emergency stocks are not large enough to cover the costs for the rice stockpile in Japan, while the benefit can be larger than the costs for the stockpile kept in Thailand when we assume the elasticity is equal to 0.1. As discussed in the main text, larger elasticity allows more flexible adjustment to shocks and leads to a smaller adverse welfare impact of quota imposition in Scenario Q.

Table A3.6: Summary statistics of simulation results for Japan (with elasticity of substitution=0.1)

Scenario	Welfare (EV)					Import price of processed rice		Calorie intake	Self-suff. rate of rice
	Min.	Mean	Max.	SD	% of GDP	Mean	SD	Min.	Mean
		[mil. US$]			Mean/GDP	[base=1.00]		[kcal/person /day]	[%]
T0	–	0	–	–	0.00	1.00	–	2,564	94.2
T1	–	4,190	–	–	0.09	0.28	–	2,621	64.3
R0	–151	1	121	34	0.00	1.01	0.05	2,561	94.2
R1	3,875	4,192	4,468	78	0.09	0.28	0.01	2,618	64.3
J0	–9,356	–401	3,374	1752	-0.01	1.00	0.02	2,458	93.4
J1	1,302	4,108	6,300	698	0.09	0.28	0.01	2,601	64.0
A0	–9,035	–401	3,402	1752	-0.01	1.02	0.05	2,464	93.4
A1	1,452	4,110	6,282	703	0.09	0.29	0.01	2,603	64.0
S	–6,296	–37	3,402	1223	0.00	0.99	0.03	2,517	91.6
M	–	5,707	–	–	0.13	0.29	–	2,611	36.0
Q	–	–17,975	–	–	-0.40	1.28	–	2,308	44.9

Table A3.7: Summary Statistics of Simulation Results for Japan (with elasticity of substitution=1.0)

Scenario	Welfare (EV)					Import price of processed rice		Calorie intake	Self-suff. rate of rice
	Min.	Mean	Max.	SD	% of GDP	Mean	SD	Min.	Mean
		[mil. US$]			Mean/GDP	[base=1.00]		[kcal/person /day]	[%]
T0	–	0	–	–	0.00	1.00	–	2,564	94.2
T1	–	5,054	–	–	0.11	0.28	–	2,622	55.9
R0	–106	–2	102	32	0.00	1.01	0.04	2,563	94.2
R1	4,746	5,056	5,469	102	0.11	0.28	0.01	2,618	55.8
J0	–18,541	–657	5,750	3009	-0.01	1.00	0.01	2,430	93.6
J1	2,235	4,980	7,355	727	0.11	0.28	0.00	2,602	55.5
A0	–18,474	–651	5,732	3005	-0.01	1.01	0.04	2,431	93.6
A1	2,335	4,980	7,319	727	0.11	0.28	0.01	2,603	55.5
S	–17,410	–506	5,732	2817	-0.01	1.00	0.04	2,448	89.4
M	–	5,708	–	–	0.13	0.29	–	2,611	36.0
Q	–	–9,665	–	–	-0.21	1.02	–	2,401	55.1

Sensitivity analysis: Volatility of productivity

There is some uncertainty in our estimates of productivity shocks shown in Table 3.3 in the main text. We conduct a sensitivity analysis with standard deviations twice as large as those used in the main text. The simulation results suggest that the standard deviations of welfare distributions in Table A3.8 become about twice as large as the original one in Table 3.4.

These doubled standard deviation cases still qualitatively support our findings drawn from the six simulations with Scenarios R0, R1, J0, J1, A0, and A1. The means of welfare under free rice trade are only marginally changed. Comparing the results of Scenarios A0 and S, the benefits of the emergency stocks are worth US$ 574 million, which is about 2.2 times as much as that expected in the original simulations. In this case, this benefit can cover the annual storage costs and capital losses.

Table A3.8: Summary statistics of simulation results for Japan (with doubled σ_r)

	Welfare (EV)					Import price of processed rice		Calorie intake	Self-suff. rate of rice
Scenario	Min.	Mean	Max.	SD	% of GDP	Mean	SD	Min.	Mean
		[mil. US$]			Mean/GDP	[base=1.00]		[kcal/person /day]	[%]
T0	–	0	–	–	0.00	1.00	–	2,564	94.2
T1	–	4,453	–	–	0.10	0.28	–	2,622	62.4
R0	–251	–0	183	53	0.00	1.03	0.09	2,560	94.2
R1	3,888	4,456	4,960	138	0.10	0.28	0.01	2,616	62.4
J0	–27,757	–1,177	5,198	3977	-0.03	1.00	0.02	2,326	92.3
J1	–3,615	4,177	7,923	1514	0.09	0.28	0.01	2,568	61.5
A0	–26,163	–1,176	5,224	3964	-0.03	1.03	0.09	2,345	92.3
A1	–2,982	4,179	7,912	1518	0.09	0.28	0.02	2,573	61.5
S	–21,768	–602	5,224	3156	-0.01	1.01	0.06	2,406	89.5
M	–	5,707	–	–	0.13	0.29	–	2,611	36.0
Q	–	–15,340	–	–	-0.34	1.20	–	2,334	46.8

Monte Carlo draws and productivity shocks

A question about our Monte Carlo simulation results may arise regarding our assumption about the distribution of productivity shocks. We plot the distribution of productivity for the sample period of our estimation (1990–2004) in Figure A3.1 and for 1961–2004 in Figure A3.2, where the productivity distributions might not be found to follow a normal distribution. Considering the upward-sloping trend of the productivity (Figure A3.3), it is better to use the rice-crop index reported by MAFF to examine the distribution (Figure A3.4). While there are two years (1945 and 1993) observed with extraordinarily low yields, the yield looks to be normally distributed, as we assume in our simulations.

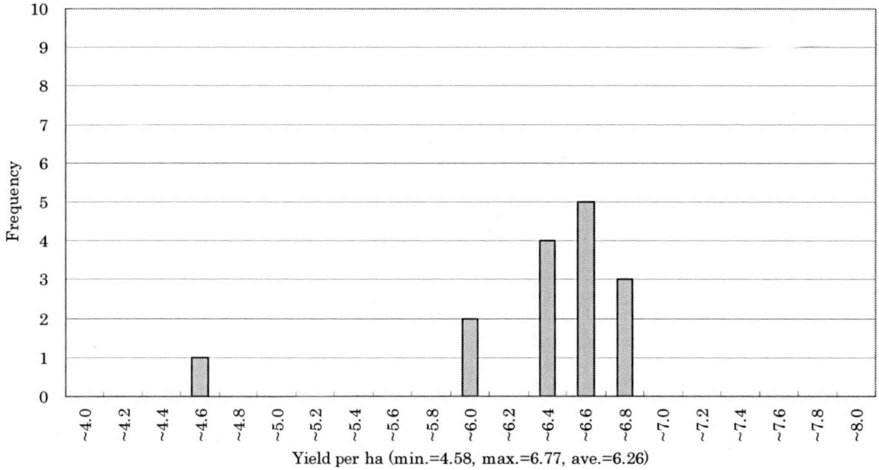

Figure A3.1: Distribution of paddy rice productivity in Japan (1990–2004) [Unit: tons/hectare]
Data source: FAOSTAT.

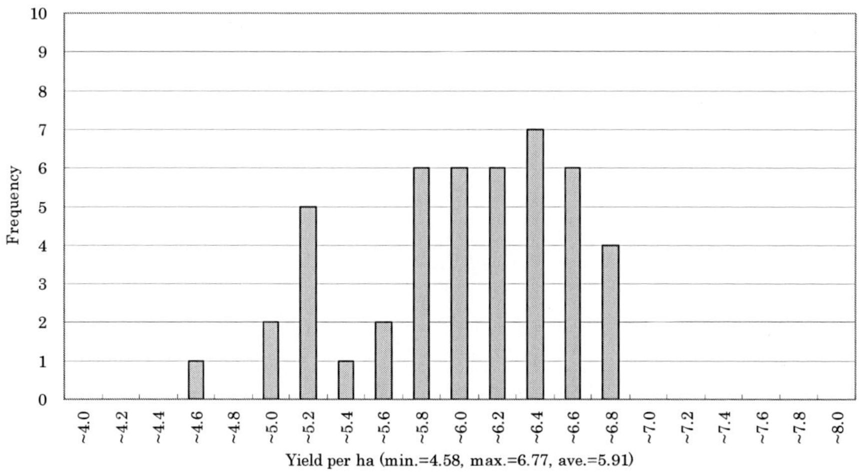

Figure A3.2: Distribution of paddy rice productivity in Japan (1961–2004) [Unit: tons/hectare]
Data source: FAOSTAT.

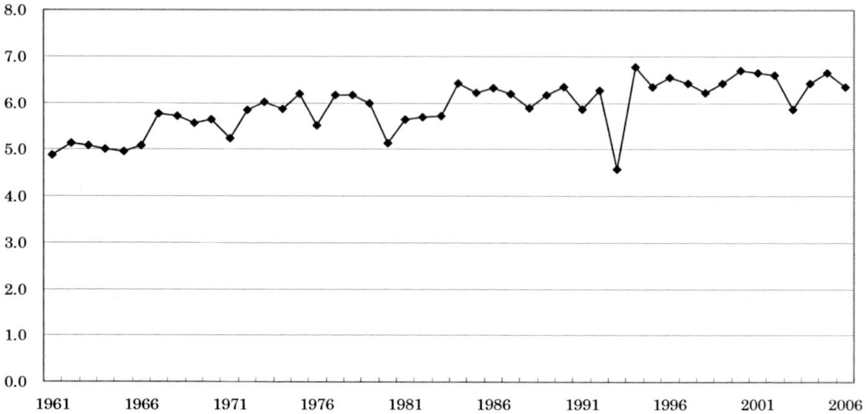

Figure A3.3: Productivity of paddy rice production in Japan [Unit: tons/hectare]
Data source: FAOSTAT.

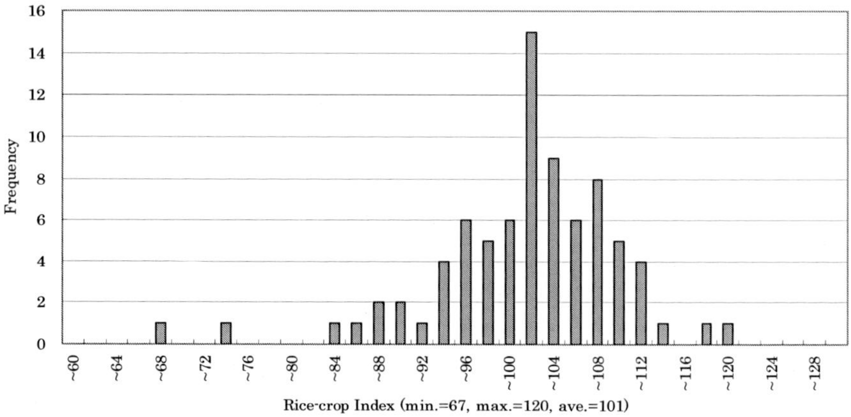

Figure A3.4: Distribution of the rice-crop index in Japan (1926–2005)
[Unit: normal yield=100]
Data source: MAFF, *Sakumotsu Tokei* [*Crop Statistics*].

Our Monte Carlo simulation generated random productivity shocks following an independent identically distributed normal distribution $N(1,\sigma_r^2)$ (Table A3.9, Figure A3.5). The summary statistics show that the means and standard deviations are consistent with our original assumption discussed in the main text.

Table A3.9: Summary statistics of the randomized productivity

	Min.	Max.	Mean	SD
Japan	0.75	1.31	1.00	0.08
China	0.91	1.08	1.00	0.03
India	0.87	1.16	1.00	0.04
Indonesia	0.94	1.07	1.00	0.02
Bangladesh	0.84	1.13	1.00	0.05
Vietnam	0.95	1.05	1.00	0.02
Thailand	0.89	1.10	1.00	0.03
Philippines	0.83	1.16	1.00	0.05
US	0.86	1.11	1.00	0.04
Australia	0.74	1.25	1.00	0.09
Rest of Asia	0.94	1.07	1.00	0.02
Other countries	0.93	1.08	1.00	0.02

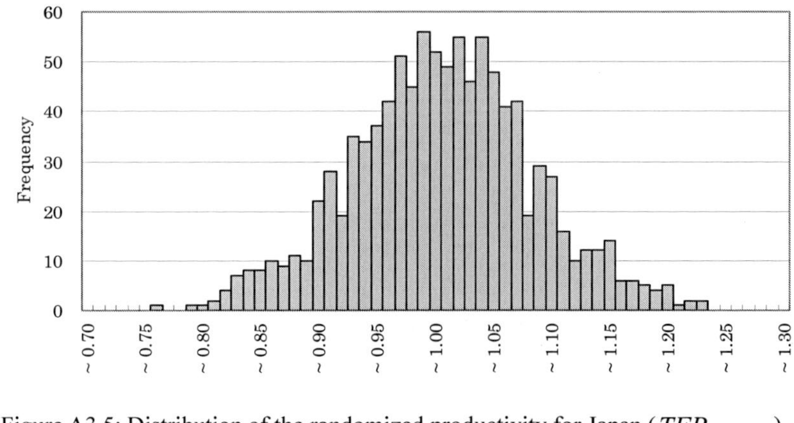

Figure A3.5: Distribution of the randomized productivity for Japan ($TFP_{PDR,JPN}$)

In our analysis, we do not consider any spatial correlations of productivity between regions. To justify this assumption, we simply examine the correlations among the residuals of the OLS model shown in Table 3.3. Table A3.10 does not indicate any systematic spatial correlations related to the distance or adjacency between regions.

Table A3.10: Correlation between the OLS residuals

	China	India	Indonesia	Bangladesh	Vietnam	Thailand	Philippines	Japan	US	Australia	Rest of Asia	Other Countries
China	–											
India	0.0	–										
Indonesia	-0.5	-0.2	–									
Bangladesh	-0.5	-0.2	0.1	–								
Vietnam	-0.3	-0.4	0.5	0.1	–							
Thailand	-0.1	-0.1	0.2	-0.2	-0.2	–						
Philippines	-0.7	-0.2	0.7	0.5	0.6	-0.1	–					
Japan	0.2	-0.2	-0.2	-0.2	-0.1	0.2	-0.1	–				
US	-0.7	-0.2	0.7	0.2	0.3	0.3	0.8	0.2	–			
Australia	-0.2	0.2	-0.4	0.3	-0.2	-0.2	0.0	-0.0	-0.3	–		
Rest of Asia	-0.6	-0.0	0.3	0.5	0.2	0.2	0.5	-0.4	0.5	-0.1	–	
Other Countries	0.1	-0.1	0.2	0.3	-0.0	-0.2	0.2	0.1	0.1	-0.3	-0.2	–

Note: the correlation is estimated by the author from the FAOSTAT.

CHAPTER FOUR

DRIVING FORCES OF THE GRAIN PRICE HIKES ON THE WORLD'S AND LDCS' MARKETS IN 2008: BACKGROUND AND LITERATURE REVIEW

TETSUJI TANAKA, NOBUHIRO HOSOE
AND HUANGUANG QIU

Background and motivation

Grain prices started rising in mid-2007, and then declined in mid-2008 (Figure 4.1). The prices of wheat, rice and maize rose by 180%, 313% and 157% at their peaks, against the average prices of 2004. Food riots occurred in around 40 developing countries with these sharp food price increases (Murphy, 2008: Figure 4.2).

In order to quieten riots down and to stabilise the regime and prices, 29 governments restricted their grain exports. Even large exporters and producers of wheat and rice such as India, Vietnam, China, and Russia imposed export bans, quotas, or taxes on the agricultural products (World Bank, 2008b).

As a result, governments and international organisations started talks about establishing urgent supports and the construction of an international food system for more stable world markets. At the 2008 G8 Summit in Japan, the governor of the World Bank called for lifting of the export restrictions, and determined to implement the following supports: (1) urgent supports for school catering and for mother and child nutrition programs; (2) offer basic substance such as seeds and fertiliser to small-scale farmers in Africa; (3) remove food export restrictions; (4) promote biofuel from non-food materials; and (5) to discuss the establishment of a virtual internationally-coordinated reserve system (G8, 2008).

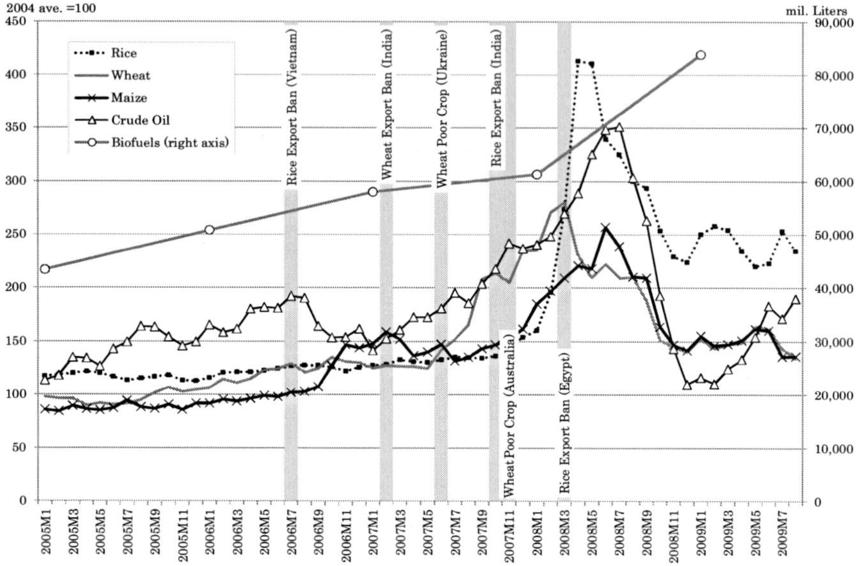

Figure 4.1: World nominal grain and oil prices and biofuel production
Data source: IMF Commodity Prices for the grain and oil prices, European Biodiesel Board for the biodiesel production, Renewable Fuel Association for the bioethanol production.

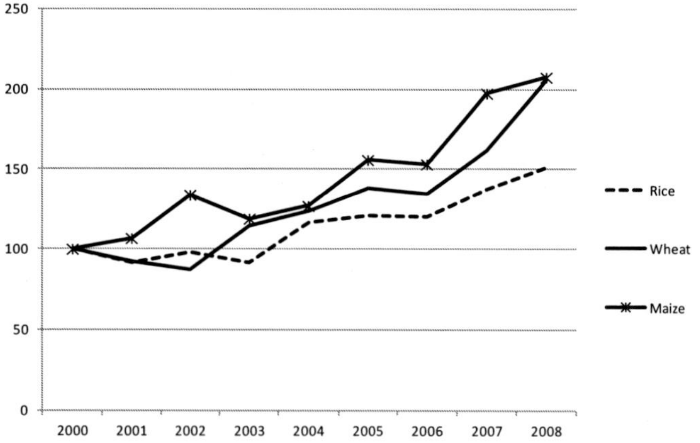

Figure 4.2: Nominal grain prices in LDCs. Data source: FAOSTAT
Note: Grain prices in 2000 are 100.

While both national and international governmental organisations make countermeasures against the food price fluctuations, economists are still struggling to uncover the factors behind the crisis, and have not yet formed a consensus view. The factors mentioned as price drivers in many reports are the increased food demand in China and India, the decline of investment in agricultural research, crop failures from extreme weather, the high oil price, biofuel production, export restrictions, the US dollar devaluation, food speculation and low world grain stock levels (von Braun et al., 2008; Abbott et al., 2008; Piesse and Thirtle, 2009). While descriptive or graphical analysis is relatively copious, quantitative research is noticeably limited.

There is also an urgent need for numerical analysis of the impact on poor regions of this world food market turmoil – some papers report that the price spikes seriously affected low-income countries. It has been a central controversy in agricultural and development economics as to whether or not high food prices increase poverty in the developing world (Aksoy and Izik-Dikmelik, 2008; Ivanic and Martin, 2008; Barrett and Dorosh, 1996; Ravallion and Lokshin, 2005). The number of net food sellers relative to that of net buyers is an important factor when discussing this question, but it is reported that there are fewer net sellers of food than net buyers in some developing countries (Christiaensen and Demery, 2007; Jayne et al., 2001).[1] Many of the papers conclude that high food prices aggravate the welfare or living standard of poor people in developing countries (Ivanic and Martin, 2008; Cudjoe et al., 2010) although Aksoy and Izik-Dikmelik (2008) demonstrate that high food prices transfer income to low-income class. Also, Arndt et al (2009) and Cudjoe et al. (2010) show the existence of price transmission of food between the global and domestic local markets and between urban and rural areas during the food crisis in 2008.

In summary, although there are many papers identifying the price drivers of the grain price rises on the global market, few papers try to estimate their impacts quantitatively. Further, analysing the impacts on the most seriously affected countries is important given that food riots occurred only in poor nations.

[1] Net sellers are defined as farm households whose quantity of a specific agricultural product sold surpasses the amount purchased in the market.

Literature review

Potential factors behind the world grain price increases

Demand growth in China and India

The economies of the first and second most populated countries, China and India, have been rapidly growing in the last decade. This has led to their meat consumption increasing, which in turn pushed up the demand for grain as feedstock (von Brown et al., 2008). However, Heady and Fan (2008) argue that China and India are self-sufficient in food. Abbott et al. (2008) insist that the countries are not major players on the world market of agriculture except that China imports soybeans and vegetable oils.

It is observed that per capita meat consumption in China has been increasing while in India it remains constant (Figure 4.3). Yet, China started notably changing its consumption pattern around 1978. In addition, the slope has been more gentle since around 1998. As Heady and Fan (2008) and Abbott et al. (2008) contend, the major grains are self-sufficient in both China and India, meaning that this factor is less likely to affect the global markets.

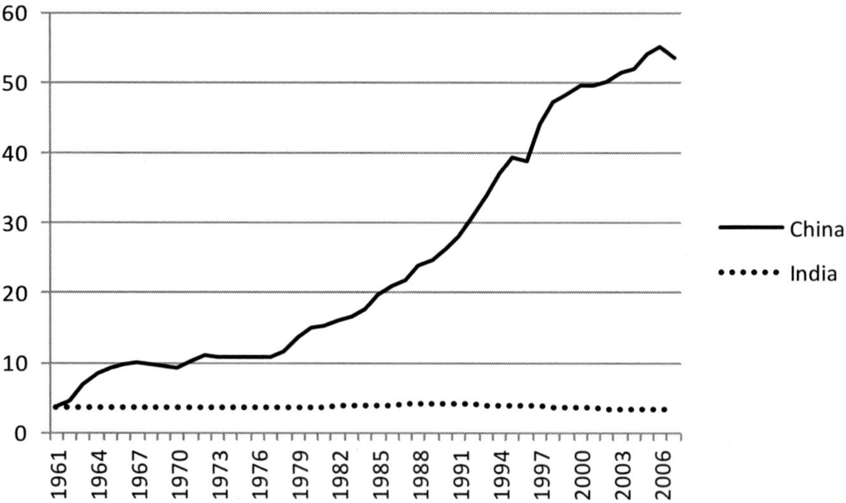

Figure 4.3: Meat consumption in China and India [Unit: kg/capita/year]
Data source: FAOSTAT

Decline of investment in agricultural research and grain productivity

Some articles maintain that the agricultural productivity growth rate has been declining and that this contributed to the food price rises (IRRI, 2008; and von Brown et al., 2008). These articles also argue that the slowdown of grain productivity occurred as a consequence of reduced public investment in agricultural research. On the other hand, Abbott et al. (2008) argue that some of the reports which mention the low level of investment in agricultural research as a critical factor actually failed to distinguish between short and long run drivers.

Figure 4.4 indicates world grain productivity from 1961 to the present. The wheat productivity seems to decline very slightly, but then grow steadily. So, it would be difficult to assert that the decreased investment in agricultural research is critically attributed to the grain price hikes in 2008.

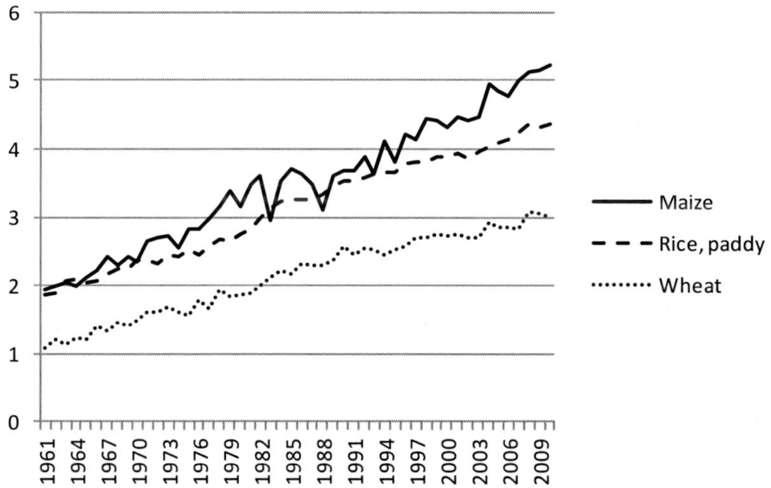

Figure 4.4: World grain productivity [Unit: tonnes/hectare]
Data source: FAOSTAT

Extreme weather pattern

Droughts, floods, and typhoons have occurred frequently and affected agricultural production in recent years. Between 2006 and 2008, severe droughts hit Australia and Ukraine, both large wheat exporting countries, which decreased their wheat production and export, affecting the world market (Mitchell, 2008; Heady and Fan, 2008). Australia and Ukraine reduced their productivity of wheat by 35% and 28% compared with 2004.[2] However, Abbott et al. (2008) and Meyers and Meyer (2008) state that the drought in Australia would not have had such a large impact under normal circumstances, but influenced grain prices with tight grain stocks.

As a matter of fact, world wheat production dropped in 2006 and 2007 (Figure 4.5) although the production did not decline dramatically – and this could support the notions above.

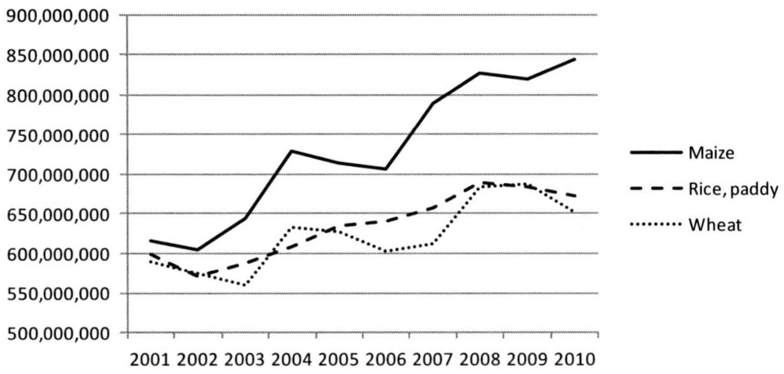

Figure 4.5: World grain production [Unit: tonnes]
Data source: FAOSTAT

Oil price hike

The price of oil rose while the grain price was spiking in this period (Figure 4.1). Increased oil prices can push up agricultural prices in several ways. First, they affect elements of modern oil-dependent food supply such as fertiliser and transport. Second, it stimulates biofuel demand, which leads to greater demand for feedstock, especially maize. Third, it depreciates the US dollar, which makes it easier for countries to import agricultural products from the US, a large exporter of grains (Piesse and Thirtle, 2009). Abbott et al. (2008) emphasise that the oil price has greater impacts on demand for corn as a component of biofuel rather than those as fertiliser and transport.

Yang et al. (2008) estimate the effects of the oil price hike on wheat and maize prices, using a world CGE model, and find that about 30% of the maize price increase is attributable to the high oil price (Table 4.1). Heady and Fan (2008) estimate the impact of fuel-related costs on US

[2] These are estimated by the author based on the data from the FAOSTAT.

farming costs between 2001 and 2007 using data from the USDA, and conclude that 87% and 54% of the price hikes can be explained by the fuel price rise.[3] Mitchell (2008) examines how the rising cost of oil impacts on the production cost of wheat and maize in the US and their transportation costs from central Illinois or Kansas City to the Gulf Ports, and finds that the petroleum price spike increased the maize price by 24%.

Increase in biofuel production

Biofuel policies in the US, Brazil and EU are widely criticised as a main driver of the food price rises. The feedstock is primarily maize, sugar cane, oilseeds and soybean. Production increased almost two-fold between 2004 and 2008 (Figure 4.1), and 33% of maize produced in the US in 2008 went to ethanol factories.[4] Many papers report that the biofuel production growth contributed in large part to the grain price hikes, especially for maize (von Brown et al., 2008; Heady and Fan, 2008; Mitchell, 2008; Abbott et al., 2008). In the US, the area of maize cultivation was expanded by 23% in 2007, and 16% of the area used for growing soybean was converted to meet the increase in maize production (Mitchell, 2008). This is observed in Figure 4.6; land-use for other crops in the US, Brazil, and EU does not show clear substitution.

Rosegrant (2008) measures the effects of the biofuel production growth using a partial equilibrium model, and concludes that it raises the wheat and rice prices by around 20% and maize prices by approximately 40%. Also, Yang et al. (2008) uses a CGE model to quantify the impacts of biofuels, and their estimates are around 25% and 45% for wheat and maize, respectively.

[3] The results in Heady and Fan (2008) are 8% and 20.3% for maize and wheat, respectively. However, they are calculated in a wrong way, and the values are estimated by the author based on the data used in the paper.

[4] It was estimated by the author based on the biofuel and maize production data from F.O. Lichts (2010) and the FAOSTAT, respectively.

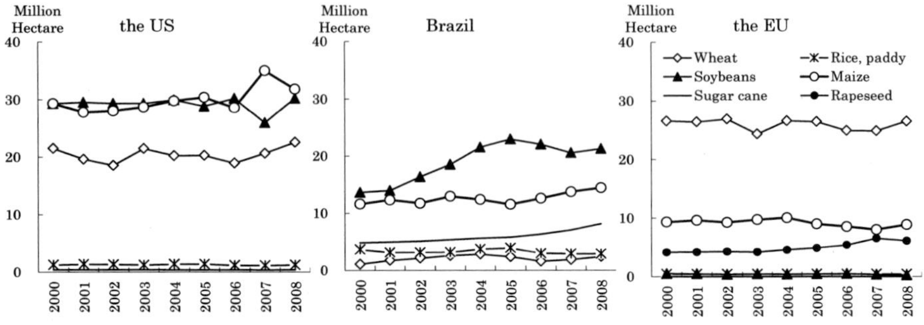

Figure 4.6: Land uses in the US, Brazil, and the EU
Data Source: FAOSTAT

Export restrictions

Restrictions on grain export were imposed by 29 countries in 2008 as a response to the grain price hikes (World Bank, 2008b). India, Vietnam, and Egypt banned rice exports, and China imposed 5% tax on its wheat, rice and maize export (Reuters, 2008; MAFF, 2008; Yang et al, 2008). Russia also put 40% tax on its wheat export (MAFF, 2008). So not only minor players in the international grain trade but also major exporting countries limited their grain exports to protect their economies.

This factor could aggravate the global grain markets (von Brown et al., 2008; IRRI, 2008; Meyers and Meyer, 2008), but is not a root cause as the countries regulated their exports as a countermeasure against the sharp price rises. Heady and Fan (2008) stress that rice export restrictions are a particularly convincing explanation because rice is thinly traded, and major rice traders regulated their exports. Charlebois (2008) employs a partial equilibrium model to estimate the effects of the export restrictions on the price of wheat, rice, and maize, and in its simulations, the rice price goes up higher than wheat and maize prices, as Heady and Fan (2008) insist.

Devaluation of the US dollar

Agricultural importing countries can save import costs through the US dollar depreciation because the US is one of the largest exporting countries of agricultural products. Since 2002, the US dollar has weakened by 30% from its peak (Piesse and Thirtle, 2009).

Abbott et al. (2008) use the USDA Economic Research Service agricultural trade-weighted index to estimate the impact of the decline in the US dollar from 2002 to 2007, and assess that the dollar depreciated by

22%, and this increased agricultural exports in the dollar value by 54%. In addition, they evaluate the effects of the deflated dollar on food price, and find that 50% of the price spike can be attributed to the US dollar devaluation, considering that the dollar fell by 30% over this period and by 56% against the euro at the maximum.

Mitchell (2008) also measures the US dollar impact on food prices citing the elasticity of dollar commodity prices with respect to the dollar exchange rate from Gilbert (1989) and Baffes (1997), which is 0.5-1.0. It argues that the dollar depreciated by 35% against the euro between January 2002 and June 2008, but the dollar devaluation against most Asian currencies was 26%. It concludes that the dollar depreciation pushed up food prices by 20%, multiplying 0.75 (taking the middle of 0.5-1.0) by 26%.

Food speculation

Speculative money could flow into food markets and increase agricultural prices (Wei, 2008; Piesse and Thirtle, 2009; Cooke and Robles, 2009; and Mitchell, 2008). Before the food price rises, the bubble burst on housing market in the US, which aggravated share markets and made commodity markets more attractive for investment, whilst the low level of grain stock encouraged speculative activity (Piesse and Thirtle, 2009). From 2002 to 2006, the number of contracts in the wheat futures market at Chicago Board of Trade quadrupled (Mitchell, 2008). Cooke and Robles (2009) also examine this issue by employing a time-series econometric model, and their results indicate that the number of futures contracts greatly explain the grain price rises.

However, Heady and Fan (2008) highlight the lack of clarity over the linkage between futures and spot prices. Abbott et al. (2008) argue that it is impossible to say clearly from the existing literature that the overall price levels were affected by speculative activities.

Low level of grain stocks

The world stock-to-utilisation rate has been declining since the late 1990s. When it is low, grain prices have upward volatility as non-commercial traders speculate on increasing prices (Piesse and Thirtle, 2009). Additionally, price changes become more sensitive to shocks as grain reserves decrease (Heady and Fan, 2008). In fact, the rate of the world grain stocks was around 30% in late 1990s, but was almost half in 2008 (Trostle, 2008). Meyers and Meyer (2008) argue that the total production and net export of grains in large grain-producing regions during the period between 2005 and 2008 did not indicate a clear drop, but the low level of the world grain reserves and increased global demand for grains tightened the markets. One reason why the low stock level occurred is that governments and private sectors try to keep limited stock to save cost with "just-in-time" inventory management. Another reason is that the recent extreme weather shocks dramatically decreased stocks (Trostle, 2008).

However, Heady and Fan (2008) emphasise that although the world maize stock level was 26% and 14% in 1990s and 2005-08, respectively, if China is taken out (as it reduced its inefficiently high stock level in 1990s) the level was 12% in both the periods,. They add that China's stock decline is not likely to have had a direct impact on international prices because major grains are self-sufficient in China as indicated before. Abbott et al. (2009) demonstrate the relationship between the stock-to-use ratio of corn and its price index. In the chart, the most of the combinations from 2007 to 2008 are outliers that imply that there are other contributory factors for the maize price rise. It should be noted that stock is not a cause, and the depletion of grain reserve is an outcome of demand exceeding supply (Piesse and Thirtle, 2009).

Table 4.1: Estimates of price rise factors

Impacts of:	on Price Rises by: Wheat [%]	Rice [%]	Maize [%]	Source	Model	Period
Export Restrictions	2	7–16	2–3	Charlebois (2008)	PE	2007, 2008
Petroleum Price Rise	18	–	31	Yang et al. (2008)	CGE	2005–08
	20	–	24	Mitchell (2008)	Cost Analysis	2002–07
Biofuels Production	22	21	39	Rosegrant (2008)	PE	2000–07
	26	–	44	Yang et al. (2008)	CGE	2005–08

Contributory factors to grain prices in LDCs

Although there are many articles in related fields, only a few studies estimate the impacts on developing economies of the potential factors behind the recent food crisis. Most of the papers assess the effects of the price rises on the living cost (Wodon et al., 2008; Wodon and Zaman, 2008; Dessus et al. (2008), but do not measure the impacts on grain prices in the LDCs' domestic markets.

Yang et al. (2008) demonstrate the validity of China's food policies during the period of the food crisis with a world CGE model. Their estimates of the impacts of the oil price hike and the emergence of biofuel on China's domestic grain prices without the preventative policies such as export tax on grains are 16.6%, 21.3% and 27.9%, and 16.7%, 16.1% and 20.6% for rice, wheat and maize, respectively. However, they only inspect two of the factors (Table 4.2).

Parra and Wodon (2008) examine the impact of oil and food price increases on living costs and food prices in Ghana, using a SAM (Table 4.2). The increase in the oil price given is 34%, which is arbitrarily set by the authors because the model is linear (if the oil price rise is 68%, the results are simply twice those in the analysis). The oil price shock raises both maize and rice prices by 6%, and increases living costs in the urban area more than in the rural area. This literature provides useful information about the extent to which people in a poor country, especially an oil-importing poor country, suffer from soaring oil prices, but it is still not clear what drove the food price hikes in poor nations.

Nganou et al. (2009) assess the impact of an oil price rise on the living expenses of the households disaggregated by income level and gender in Kenya, using a SAM (Table 4.2). With a 25% oil price shock, the price of maize goes up by 9%. The increase in the cost of living is estimated at 9%.[5] This study employs the same method as the one used by Parra and Wodon (2008), but the difference of the effect by oil price changes between the two papers is considered to be attributed to the difference of coefficients of SAMs between the two countries, which are calibrated from the data.

Table 4.2: Impact estimation on grain prices in developing countries by existing literature

Impacts of:	on Prices of:			Source	Model	Period	Region
	Wheat [%]	Rice [%]	Maize [%]				
Petroleum Price Rise	21.3	16.6	27.9	Yang et al. (2008)	CGE	2005-08	China
	–	–	9.1	Nganou et al. (2009)	SAM	2001	Kenya
	–	6.1	6.4	Parra and Wodon (2008)	SAM	2005	Ghana
Biofuels Production	16.1	16.7	20.6	Yang et al. (2008)	CGE	2005–08	China

[5] Nganou et al. (2009) do not explicitly describe if the price changes are nominal or real. If it is nominal, the price of maize is almost constant in real term.

Implications to our research

We have reviewed many articles for the two topics in this section: identifying factors which raise grain prices on the world market; and those which affect them in developing regions. As discussed above, consensus has not yet been reached on either issue. So, we will investigate scenario factors based on the literature survey with the CGE model described in Chapter 2.

For the first subject, nine primary factors were investigated. Some were discounted for various reasons. Among these, increased demand in China and India and the decline of investment in agricultural research can be classified as long-run factors, not so relevant for this study as our focus is on grain price rises over only one or two years – although they might have had slight impacts on the prices. The model used for this research is a real economic model, which does not explicitly consider financial markets. Hence, financial-related factors such as financial speculation and the US dollar devaluation are excluded as scenario factors in the analysis.[6] As Wright (2011) insists, when grain stock levels are quite low, price responses to the shocks are large. This is examined in the sensitivity analysis in which the elasticity of substitution in the Armington function is changed to a smaller value. Therefore, we consider the extreme weather, oil price hike, increase in biofuel production and export restrictions as shocks.

As we have seen, impoverished countries suffered from the food crisis more severely than advanced nations. However, the regions focused on in previous work estimating the effects are China, Kenya and Ghana, none of which are included in LDCs.[7] What is more, only the two factors, oil price increase and biofuels, are investigated in the analyses. It is beneficial to evaluate the impacts on the individual countries of LDCs, but LDCs are 50 regions, and around 10 large grain-producing and exporting countries need to be considered in the model. With so many nations (i.e. many variables), the simulations will cause computational difficulties. Further, when international policies are decided in an intergovernmental meeting like the G8 summit in 2009, it is important to know which factor has what degree of impact on the LDCs as a whole. For these reasons, we will evaluate the

[6] Real economy is the economy in which actually goods and services are produced in contrast with financial economy.

[7] The definition of LDCs follows the one by the United Nations. The LDCs are currently 50 countries. There are three criterion; low income, human resource weakness, and economic vulnerability. See the UN website at http://www.nationsonline.org/oneworld/least_developed_countries.htm.

aggregated impacts of these factors on LDCs' economies, using the CGE model explained in Chapter 2.

Conclusion

In 2008, food prices on the world market increased sharply, and food riots occurred in many developing countries. To isolate domestic markets, many national governments imposed bans on their grain exports, which accelerated the price rises by tightening the global markets. While the G8 reached agreements on countermeasures against the constrained food markets, the real causes have not yet been fully identified by academic experts. Although destitute countries suffered from the price spikes more acutely, the research is very scarce. In this chapter, nine potential factors of the food price hikes were discussed and some removed from consideration. Demand increases in China and India and the decline of investment in agricultural research and grain productivity are long-term contributory factors for these short-term price spikes. Our CGE model is a real economic model that cannot capture the impacts of financial factors. Low grain stock levels which could make grain demand less price-elastic will be analysed in the sensitivity tests. We will use the model to assess the effects of the remaining four factors (crop failures, export restrictions, oil price hike and biofuel production) on the world grain markets and the LDC grain markets.

CHAPTER FIVE

DRIVING FORCES OF THE GRAIN PRICE HIKES ON THE WORLD'S AND LDCS' MARKETS IN 2008: MODEL, DATA AND SCENARIOS

TETSUJI TANAKA, NOBUHIRO HOSOE AND HUANGUANG QIU

Introduction

The previous chapter provided a literature review of the grain price rises in the global and LDC markets. This chapter establishes the methodology for the two studies. First, models introduced in the preceding chapter are reviewed, and our model is explained. Second, the data for the newly created maize and biofuel sectors, elasticity and grain prices, are described. Finally, the simulation scenarios are delineated.

Model

Model Review

Rosegrant (2008) applies the International Model for Policy Analysis of Agricultural Commodities and Trade (IMPACT) model developed by the International Food Policy Research Institute (IFPRI) for estimating the impacts of biofuel production on the prices of crops. The model has 115 regions and at least five agricultural commodities.[1] An advantage of the model is the fine disaggregation of country that can reflect small changes

---

[1] Rosegrant (2008) does not show the number of commodities in the model. See Rosegrant et al. (2008) for the description on the structure of the IMPACT model.

in the countries' situations. However, it ignores the influence of an increase in biofuel production on oil demand and price which affects food production, especially maize, through the cost expansion of transport and fertiliser.

Both Nagnough (2008) and Parra and Wodon (2008) employ SAM models based on Kenya and Ghana to inspect oil price effects on the economies. The models they use are price-based SAM models extended from a traditional SAM model. The household data is disaggregated by gender and detailed income-class, and the impacts on income distribution can be identified. However, these are linear models that do not describe behaviour changes in response to price variations, and so they may fail to give a precise estimation, especially in situations where prices are greatly affected by shocks.

Yang et al. (2008) use a world CGE model to discuss the effects of the Chinese government's policy against the global food price spikes, and to measure the impacts of biofuel production and the rise in oil price. One strength is that it is a recursive dynamic model, from 2006 to 2008, which makes it possible to simulate food price changes by year – and so the path of the price movements can be identified. Nevertheless, it assumes that there is a substitution between capital stock and energy in the production structure, but this is not likely to occur in the short term.

Model Structure

A single-country CGE model used in Devarajan et al. (1990) is extended to a multi-country model for this study. We explain the model only briefly here since it was described in detail in Chapter 2.

Each sector has a perfectly competitive profit-maximizing firm with Leontief production function for gross output. While labour is mobile across all sectors but immobile across regions, capital stocks and farmland are assumed to be immobile between all the sectors and regions. The value-added composite made of these factors are combined with intermediate inputs to produce gross output, which is allocated between domestic good supply and composite exports by a constant elasticity of transformation (CET) function. The composite exports are further decomposed into outbound shipping to individual regions with the CET technology. Similarly, the domestic goods and composite imports made of inbound shipping from various regions are combined into composite goods with a constant elasticity of substitution (CES) function following Armington (1969). The composite imports are generated with imports shipped from various regions. The elasticities of the CES and CET functions of imports and exports are quoted from the GTAP database.

A representative household maximizes its utility subject to its budget constraint. The consumption is determined by the two-stage budgeting. First, the household considers a trade-off among various food-related goods. Its food consumption is aggregated into a food composite with a CES function, whose elasticity of substitution is assumed to be 0.1, following Tanaka and Hosoe (2011b). At the first stage, the household considers a trade-off among the food composite and the other goods.

Data

Regional and sector aggregations

The GTAP database ver. 7.1 has 113 regions and 57 sectors that are aggregated focusing on large producing and exporting countries of agricultural commodities for the regional aggregation and agricultural/food and energy sectors for the sector aggregation (Table 5.1). Table 5.1 expresses the aggregation for the research on LDCs. In the study to identify the factors underlying the world grain price increases, "LDCs" is incorporated with "Rest of the World." Maize, bioethanol and biodiesel sectors are not displayed in the original dataset although they are included in it. The sectors are indispensable for the two analyses, and are made following the approach of Taheripour et al. (2008), which is explained in the next section.

Table 5.1: Country and sector aggregations

Country	Sector
Australia	Paddy Rice
Argentina	Wheat
Brazil	Maize**
China	Other Grains
Egypt	Oilseeds
India	Other Agriculture
Phillipines	Sugar Cane and Beet
Russia	Processed Rice
Thailand	Other Foods
Ukraine	Coal
USA	Gas
Vietnam	Electricity
LDCs*	Crude Oil
EU	Petroleum
Rest of the World	Bioethanol**
	Biodiesel**
	Transport
	Others

Note: * is included in "Rest of the World" in the topic on the world food prices.** are introduced into the GTAP database.

Splitting Sectors in the GTAP Database

Maize is not distinguished but included as part of other grains in the original GTAP database version 7.1. Neither bioethanol nor biodiesel is identified in the original database either. Therefore, we create these three sectors by splitting the other grains and the oil sectors (Table 5.1). Considering the relative size of the maize production vis-à-vis the other grains (i.e., cereals other than rice and wheat) reported in the FAOSTAT, we split the row and column of the other grains in the original social accounting matrix (SAM), constructed on the basis of the GTAP database. The column of the original oil sector and biofuels trade are split based on the cost component information and trade flows provided by Taheripour et al. (2008) with the biofuels production and price quoted for 2004 from various sources (Table 5.2). The row of the original oil sector is split into the share of oil and biofuels consumption. As these new inputs unbalance the SAM, we adjust it by solving a constrained matrix problem, à la Hosoe et al. (2010, Ch. 4).

Table 5.2: Splitting maize and biofuels sectors

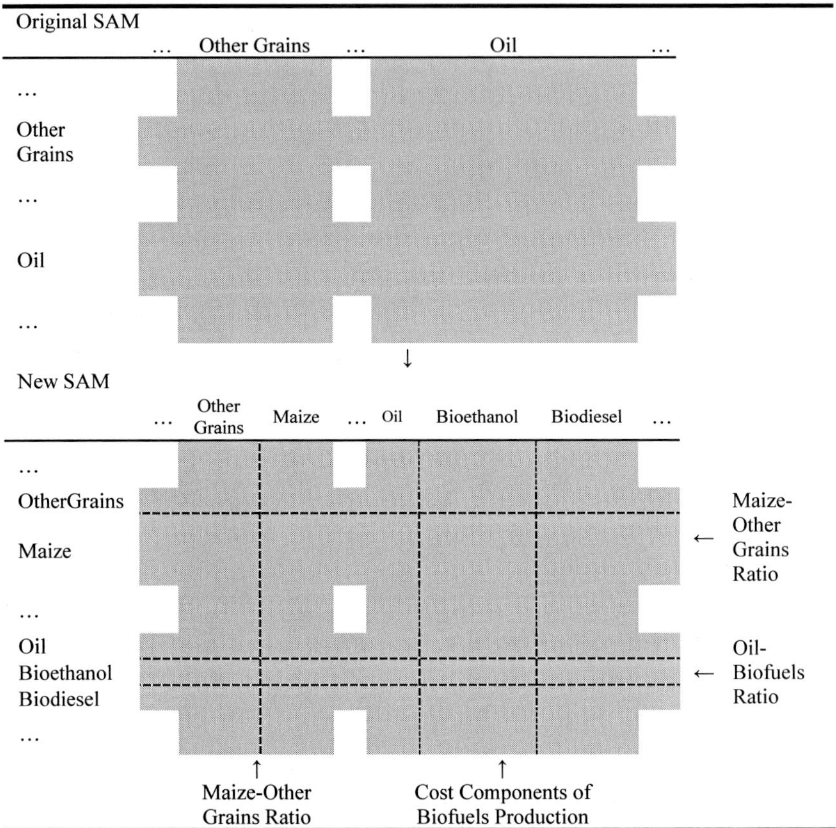

Note: Maize-other grains ratio is computed by the FAOSTAT. The cost components of biofuels production and biofuels trade are reported by Taheripour et al. (2008). Data sources of other biofuels data are shown in Table 5.3. "Other Grains" sector in the original GTAP database includes all cereal grains such as maize, soybeans, and barley except rice and wheat.

Table 5.3: Biofuel data sources

Data	Fuel Type	Data Source
Production	Bio-ethanol	F.O.Licht, World Ethanol & Biofuels Report
	Biodiesel	National Biodiesel Board (the US) http://www.biodiesel.org/pdf_files/fuelfactsheets/Production_Graph_Slide.pdf European Biodiesel Board (the EU) http://www.ebb-eu.org/prev_stats_production.php
Price	Bio-ethanol & biodiesel	US Department of Energy"The Alternative Fuel Price Report," March 23, 2004. http://www.afdc.energy.gov/afdc/pdfs/afpr_3_23_04.pdf

Elasticity parameters

The values for the elasticity of substitution are quoted mainly from the GTAP database ver. 7.1 (Table 5.4). The elasticity for maize is applied at the same value as that for the other grains sector from which the maize sector is split. Regarding the Armington elasticity and the elasticity of a value-added composite for biofuel sectors, the values of the petroleum sector are applied. Since 1.0 is used for the elasticity of substitution among energy goods in the GTAP-E(nergy) model, we put 1.0 for an energy composite good, and 2.0 for a liquid energy composite considering the substitutability (Burniaux and Truong, 2002). These values are the same in both the production and consumption structure. As in Chapter 3, the elasticity of food composite good for household is 0.1.[2]

[2] See the appendix in Chapter 3 for the elasticity survey.

Table 5.4: Elasticity parameter values in the model

Sector	Production				Consumption		
	Armington	Value Added	Liquid Energy	Non-liquid Energy	Food	Liquid Energy	Non-liquid Energy
Paddy Rice	5.1	0.2	2.0	1.0		-	-
Wheat	4.4	0.2	2.0	1.0		-	-
Maize	1.3	0.2	2.0	1.0		-	-
Other Grains	1.3	0.2	2.0	1.0		-	-
Oilseeds	2.5	0.2	2.0	1.0	0.1	-	-
Other Agriculture	2.2	0.2	2.0	1.0		-	-
Sugar Cane and Beet	2.7	0.2	2.0	1.0		-	-
Processed Rice	2.6	1.1	2.0	1.0		-	-
Other Foods	2.4	1.1	2.0	1.0		-	-
Coal	3.0	0.2	2.0	1.0	-	-	
Gas	17.2	0.2	2.0	1.0	-	-	
Electricity	2.8	1.3	2.0	1.0	-	-	
Crude Oil	5.2	0.2	2.0	1.0	-		1.0
Petroleum	2.1	1.3	2.0	1.0	-		
Bioethanol	2.1	1.3	2.0	1.0	-	2.0	
Biodiesel	2.1	1.3	2.0	1.0	-		
Transport	1.9	1.7	2.0	1.0	-	-	-
Others	2.5	1.3	2.0	1.0	-	-	-

Data Source: the GTAP database ver. 7.1 for the Armington and value added elasticities.

Price data

The actual data for price changes on the global grain market is used to compare against simulated price variations. The IMF commodity prices are cited for the nominal world prices of wheat, rice and maize, which are deflated by the core inflation data from the IMF World Economic Outlook 2009. The real actual prices are standardised by the average of the prices in 2004, which is the base year of the simulations. The mean values of the real commodity indices for one year (2008) are used as actual price variations in the simulations. Since the IMF Commodity Prices assumes that the export price of the largest exporting country of a commodity represents the world price (these are the US for wheat and maize and Thailand for rice) we follow this method to gauge the world prices of wheat, rice and maize in the model.

Nominal grain prices in LDCs are cited from the FAOSTAT. The prices are deflated and weighted-averaged by the data on inflation and consumption of individual LDCs from the World Bank and FAOSTAT for the grain prices in LDCs, respectively. Then, the values are standardised by the average of the wheat, rice and maize prices for 2004. The consumer's prices of wheat, rice and maize in LDCs in the model are used as the simulated impacts on grain prices in the region.

Scenarios

The four types of shocks are considered individually in Scenarios C, R, P, and B. The fifth Scenario A considers all four at once (Table 5.5). Even if we take account of all these four major real-side factors in Scenario A, the estimated price rises of these crops will fall short of the actual price rise. This gap would be attributed to other factors.

In Scenario C (crop failures), we simulate the bad wheat crops in Australia and Ukraine that occurred in 2007 (Table 5.6). These shocks are given to the total factor productivity parameter in the gross output production function. Scenario R (export restrictions) captures the impact of the export restrictions on crops. While many countries set some type of export restrictions such as bans, quotas, and taxes, we focus on the actions by the six major countries with market shares larger than 1% of the world exports. We assume a 95% cut of exports as an approximation of export bans to avoid computational difficulty in our CGE model, where a nested CES structure is used to describe the bilateral trade patterns. In Scenario P (petroleum), an oil price hike of 126% is assumed. This price rise is generated by the imposition of export taxes on crude oil at the same rate by all oil exporters. Scenario B (biofuels) is designed to evaluate the impact of bioethanol production from maize and sugarcane in the US and Brazil, respectively, and that of biodiesel production from oilseeds in the EU. We set the bioethanol and biodiesel production at the actual level in 2008 leveraged by production subsidies for these two sectors.

Table 5.5: Scenario table

Scenario	Scenario Factor			
	Crop Failures	Export Restrictions	Petroleum Price Rise	Biofuels Emergence
Base run	–	–	–	–
C	yes	–	–	–
R	–	yes	–	–
P	–	–	yes	–
B	–	–	–	yes
A	yes	yes	yes	yes

Table 5.6: Crop and its related market shocks in 2007/2008

Scenario Factor	Country	Sector	Type of Shock	Magnitude
Crop Failures	Australia	Wheat	Productivity Decline	35%
	Ukraine	Wheat		28%
Export Restrictions	Argentina	What	Export Tax	28%
		Maize		25%
	China	Wheat		20%
		Rice		5%
		Maize		
	Egypt	Rice	Export Ban	95% ExportCut*
	India	Wheat		
		Rice		
	Vietnam	Rice		
	Russia	Wheat	Export Tax	40%
Crude Oil Price Hike	World	Crude Oil	Export Price Rise	126%
Biofuel Productions	Brazil	Bioethanol	Increase of Production	162%
	USA			255%
	EU	Biodiesel		345%

Data Source: FAOSTAT, Sharma (2011), USDA (2008), and World Bank (2008a).
Note: Export ban is approximated with imposition of a 95% export quotas.

Conclusion

We have critically reviewed the models discussed in the existing literature, and explained the advantages and disadvantages of the model. Based on these, our CGE model was designed and described. The regional and sectoral aggregations are shown, but the original GTAP database does not have maize, bioethanol and biodiesel sectors necessary in this research. They have been introduced to the database for this research. Most of the elasticity parameters are quoted from the GTAP database, but the elasticity of substitution among food products for a household is cited from existing studies, and the GTAP-E model is followed for the elasticity of an energy composite, which is doubled for liquid energy goods. Actual food prices, which will be compared with the estimated price variations, are adduced from the IMF Commodity Prices and FAOSTAT. They are deflated by inflation data from the IMF Economic Outlook and the World Bank and standardized by 2004, which is the base year of the simulations. The export prices of wheat and maize in the US and that of rice in Thailand in the model are utilised as the calculated world prices as for the IMF Commodity Prices. Finally, we explained the shocks given and the scenarios.

CHAPTER SIX

DRIVING FORCES OF THE GRAIN PRICE HIKES ON THE WORLD'S AND LDCS' MARKETS IN 2008: SIMULATION RESULTS AND POLICY IMPLICATIONS

TETSUJI TANAKA, NOBUHIRO HOSOE AND HUANGUANG QIU

Introduction

Chapters 4 and 5 presented literature reviews and the methodology. This chapter shows the estimated impacts of the four real-side shocks (crop failures, export restrictions, oil price hike and biofuel production) on grain prices in global markets and LDCs. Firstly, the results of the world grain prices are explained. Secondly, the outcome of the shocks on LDCs is shown, and policy implications are made on the basis of the estimation. Thirdly, a set of sensitivity analyses will be presented in the Appendix.

Results: the impacts on the world grain markets

Of the four factors, crop failure is the largest contributor to wheat price rises, although it affects the other markets little (Table 6.1). Although Ukraine was often quoted as one of the major causes of wheat shortage, it does not actually give any sizable shock to the world export supply (Table 6.2). It should also be noted that this price rise is brought about through the contraction of wheat exports, not through any sizable loss of production (Scenario C). Export restrictions directly cut wheat exports, raising its price further (Scenario R). On the other hand, the US dollar appreciates due to the petroleum price rise; this leads to a moderate rise of the dollar-denominated wheat price (Scenario P).

Table 6.1: Decomposition analysis of the grain price hikes in the world market [Unit: percent]

Scenario	Changes [%]			Share of Impact [%]		
	Wheat	Rice	Maize	Wheat	Rice	Maize
Actual Price Rises	**87**	**164**	**79**	**100**	**100**	**100**
C (Crop Failure)						
Price	**7.2**	**−0.1**	**−0.2**	**9.6**	**−0.1**	**−0.3**
Production	−0.2	−0.0	−0.0			
Exports	−5.3	−0.1	−0.1			
R (Export Restrictions)						
Price	**3.6**	**14.2**	**0.2**	**4.9**	**9.3**	**0.4**
Production	0.2	−0.1	−0.1			
Exports	−2.8	−30.0	−1.4			
P (Petroleum Price Rise)						
Price	**3.0**	**0.1**	**3.3**	**4.0**	**0.0**	**4.9**
Production	−0.0	−0.0	0.3			
Exports	−0.3	0.1	0.5			
B (Biofuel Production)						
Price	**−1.4**	**−1.5**	**8.1**	**−1.9**	**−1.0**	**12.1**
Production	−0.2	−0.3	1.8			
Exports	−0.2	−0.7	−2.8			
Interactive Effects	**1.4**	**−0.5**	**−0.3**	**1.9**	**−0.4**	**−0.5**
A (All)						
Price	**13.9**	**12.1**	**11.1**	**18.5**	**8.0**	**16.6**
Production	−0.1	−0.4	1.9			
Exports	−8.4	−28.8	−3.5			
The Rest (Actual - A)	**61.1**	**139.9**	**55.9**	**81.5**	**92.0**	**83.4**

Note: all the price changes are in real term.

Table 6.2: Changes of grain exports in Scenario A [Unit: percent]

	Paddy Rice	Processed Rice	Wheat	Maize
Australia	0.0	0.0	-7.7	0.0
Brazil	0.0	0.0	0.1	1.1
Ukraine	0.0	0.0	-1.4	0.0
China	0.2	0.5	-0.1	0.0
India	-0.4	-19.1	-1.6	0.1
Thailand	0.0	4.4	0.0	0.1
Vietnam	0.0	-15.9	0.0	0.0
USA	3.0	1.9	0.8	-4.0
Argentina	-1.2	0.0	-0.5	-1.2
Phillipines	0.0	0.0	0.0	0.0
Russia	0.0	0.0	-2.0	0.0
Egypt	0.0	-3.2	0.0	0.0
EU	0.6	0.4	3.2	0.2
Rest of the World	0.3	1.2	0.9	0.1

The export restrictions are the primal cause of the rice price rise (Table 6.1). This price rise is particularly sharp, partly because the international rice market is far thinner than for other crops and partly because export restrictions cover rice exports more widely than other crops exports. Among the export restrictions on rice, those made by Vietnam and India are particularly significant in reducing the world market supply (Table 6.2). The price of rice measured by the Thai export price in US dollars is not much affected by the oil price increase as the Thai baht is devalued against the US dollar by the high oil price.

With few countries imposing export restrictions on maize, the price of maize is not increased by this, although the petroleum price rise and the emergence of biofuel do contribute to increases in the maize price. The oil price hike stimulates demand for maize through the use of biofuel as a substitute. However, the impact of biofuel production is twice as much as that of the oil price spike, using much maize as a feedstock and cutting its export by the US.

In sum, the result of the simulation for the wheat price could partly support Abbott et al. (2008) and Meyers and Meyer (2008) who indicate that the drought in Australia alone would not have had a large impact on the international wheat price, but only with the depletion of grain stocks. However, crop failures are the most critical factor among the four we are considering. As Wright (2011) argues, the impacts of these shocks tend to be large when the crop reserve level is very low, which makes the crop demand less price-elastic. Although we do not explicitly consider such stock behaviour in our CGE model, in the Appendix we do assume a smaller elasticity for agricultural products to approximate the situation. The results do not show significant difference in the robustness tests.

Export restrictions hit the rice market significantly, but not the wheat and maize markets. This finding is similar to Charlebois (2008), and could support the argument made by Heady and Fan (2008) that export restrictions push up the rice price especially, because the major players in the international rice market restrict their exports, and rice is thinly traded on the international market.

In Scenario P, bioethanol production in the US increases by just 7%, which is different from the finding in the work by Abbott et al. (2008). In the simulation, the oil price rise increases the price of transportation in the US by 17%. This estimate is only a little smaller than the calculation by Mitchell (2008). While the fuel-related impacts on maize and wheat production by Heady and Fan (2008) are 35.5% and 27.8%, respectively, in our simulation the high oil price increases the producer prices by 4.7% for maize and 4.6% for wheat. So, regarding the oil price, our estimation is generally smaller than in these past reports. The sensitivity tests of the elasticity of energy substitution also do not indicate large differences from the original decomposition analysis (Tables A6.6 and A6.7).

Given that there was little farm-land conversion from maize to rice or wheat during the period with which we are concerned (Figure 4.6), we put the farm-land immobility assumption into the model. Therefore only the maize price is increased by biofuel production, although the prices of wheat and rice do rise in Rosegrant (2008) and Yang et al. (2008). While a number of past studies report that biofuel is a main driver of the maize price, our estimates are much smaller. The maize export data from the FAOSTAT shows that the share of the US maize export in the world total exports between 2000 and 2008 ranges between almost 50% and 60%. There do not seem to have been major fluctuations in the US maize export during grain price hikes, but the shares in 2007 and 2008 were slightly smaller than in 2006 (Figures 6.1 and 6.2). Although the US import of maize increased between 2006 and 2008, the share of the world total maize import went up only from 0.2% to 0.5%, which cannot constitute a large shake on the global market (Figure 6.3). These facts partly support the result of Scenario B.

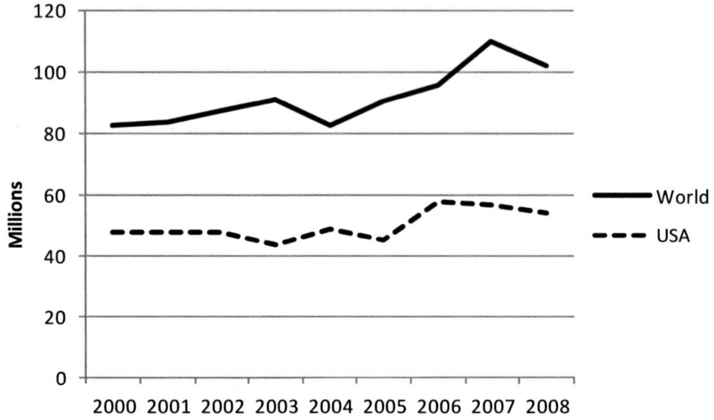

Figure 6.1: World maize export and maize export from the US [Unit: million tonnes]
Data source: FAOSTAT

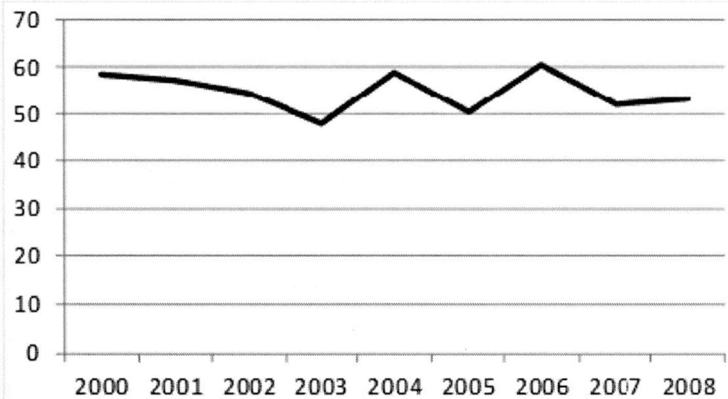

Figure 6.2: Share of maize export from the US in the world total export [Unit: percent]
Data source: FAOSTAT

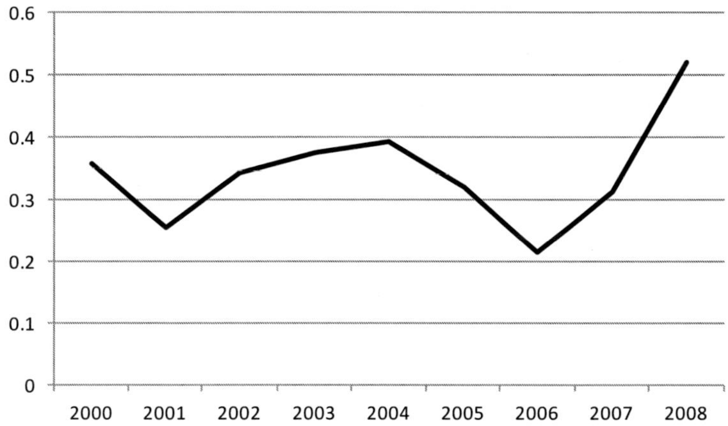

Figure 6.3: Share of maize import by the US to the world total import [Unit: percent]
Data source: FAOSTAT

As explained above, our simulations show that only the maize price is increased by biofuel while our result disagrees with the consensus that biofuel is responsible for much of the global maize price hike. This is partly because there was no serious demand-supply shock for maize except biofuel, if financial factors are assumed not to be significant causes. What is more, a huge amount of feedstock was input into the production in the US in 2008, and this information could have led to misunderstanding because the maize production in the US indicates a gradual increase from 2000 to 2008 which partly but not entirely covered the feedstock of bioethanol, and alleviated the maize export reduction (Figures 6.1 and 6.2). However, the robustness analyses with the smaller value of the elasticity of factor substitution (which substantially influenced labour mobility because other factors are immobile across sectors) demonstrate that biofuel explains 33% of the price increase in maize (Table A6.3). If it is assumed that in agricultural sectors labour behaviour does not respond to wage in the short term (one or two years), the estimate of maize produced from our model could be closer to those from Rosegrant (2008) and Yang et al. (2008) even though the small elasticity of 0.1 implies sluggish labour mobility.

The circumstance of the low level of the world grain stocks is expressed by a robustness test (Table A6.2), but there is little evident dissimilarity with the original results. This is contrary to the expectation of

Timmer (2008), Piesse and Thirtle (2009) and Meyers and Meyer (2008) that the depletion of grain stocks made the grain demand less price-elastic. This suggests that the reasoning by Heady and Fan (2008) and Abbott et al. (2009) that the world grain reserves did not affect the international market seriously can be substantiated in part by our simulations. However, as Piesse and Thirtle (2009) maintain, sufficient grain stocks might discourage speculative actions. The results of the sensitivity test could highlight that an important role of grain reserves is to prevent speculation.

Results: the impacts on the LDCs' grain markets

The poor wheat harvests in Australia and Ukraine had the greatest impact of all four factors on increasing the LDC wheat price (Table 6.3). The wheat price is boosted by export restrictions to almost the same level as by crop failures. While the international wheat price rises with the petroleum price hike, the LDC wheat price goes slightly down. This is because the regions rely on import for around 30% of their wheat supply, and their currencies are appreciated by the oil price hike because some of the LDCs are oil-rich countries (Figure 6.4).

Table 6.3: Decomposition analysis of grain price hikes in LDCs

Scenario	Change in Price [%]			Share of Impact [%]		
	Wheat	Rice	Maize	Wheat	Rice	Maize
Actual Price Rises	66.0	30.0	63.0	100.0	100.0	100.0
Impact of;						
C (Crop Failure)	5.8	-0.1	-0.1	8.8	-0.3	-0.2
R (Export Restrictions)	5.0	9.8	-1.1	7.5	32.7	-1.7
P (Petroleum Price Rise)	-1.4	7.4	5.9	-2.1	24.7	9.3
B (Biofuel Production)	-0.2	-0.3	0.2	-0.4	-1.1	0.3
Interactive Effects	1.5	2.0	-0.3	2.2	6.6	-0.5
A (All)	10.7	18.8	4.6	16.2	62.5	7.3
The Rest (Actual Price Rises - A)	55.3	11.3	58.4	83.8	37.5	92.7

Note: all the price changes are in real term.

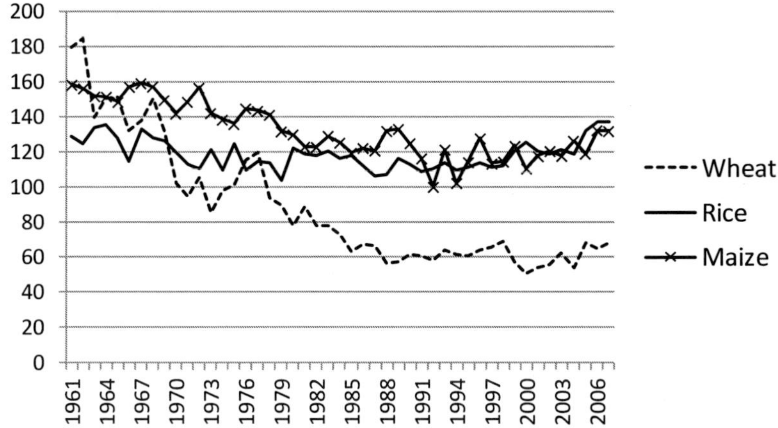

Figure 6.4: Self-sufficiency rate of grains in LDCs (production/consumption) [Unit: percent]
Data source: FAOSTAT

As in the analysis of the global grain market, the export restrictions were found to be the most influential of the factors in pushing up the LDC rice price. The oil price hike also increases the rice price in LDCs, while the wheat price declines because rice is self-sufficient in the regions, and these countries do not exploit the advantage of their currencies' appreciation by the high oil price, but do suffer from the rising international rice price transmitted from their rice export. However, the rice price is not greatly influenced by bad crops and biofuel production.

The LDC maize price is not increased by export restrictions because only a few countries impose restrictions on their maize export. However, since the real income in LDCs is restrained by general commodity inflation, the negative income effect lowers the maize price in Scenario R. The petroleum price spike causes an increase in income, stimulates the general demand for commodities, and raises commodity prices, because LDCs do not take advantage of their currencies' appreciation as a result of the insulated domestic market. On the other hand, due to the isolation of the LDCs' maize market, the domestic maize markets are only marginally affected by the higher global maize price caused by biofuel production.

In Scenario A, the prices of wheat, rice and maize rise by around 11%, 19% and 5%. Over half the price rise in rice is accounted for by the four factors, but these four real-side factors explain the increased prices of wheat and maize by merely 16% and 7%. Hence, for wheat and maize, the remaining 80%-plus are attributed to other factors. Most of the sensitivity tests shown in the Appendix find the results robust for wheat and maize. Yet, when changing the elasticity of substitution for a value-added composite good from 0.2 to 0.1 or 1.0 for agricultural sectors, the explanatory shares of rice are very wide-ranging., between 35% and 88%. Considering that the grain price spikes last for one or two-years, which is short for labour mobility across sectors, the parameter could be smaller than the 0.2 applied for the original calculations. Also, it should be noted that comparing the results between Tables 6.3 and A6.10, the impact shares of rice for Scenario R and P increase by 47% and 30% respectively, which suggests that the effect of the export restrictions is more likely to be under-estimated by the changed elasticity than the effect of the high oil price.[1]

The oil price hike during the period from 2004 to 2008 raised the prices of rice and maize by 7.4% and 5.9%, but did not change the price of wheat very much. The prices of rice and maize are affected more in the LDCs' markets than in the world's markets. In Nganou et al. (2009) and Parr and Wodon (2008), increases of 25% and 34% in the oil price push the maize price,up by 9% and 6% respectively. Both studies employ linear models, so if the results of the two papers are applied the price rises in maize are 45% and 22% compared to 126% used in our analysis. These estimates are much higher than the ones estimated in this book. This is primarily because we use a non-linear model, which is more flexible in adjusting to the shocks.

It is difficult to explain why an oil price hike and biofuel affect grain prices because Yang et al (2008) do not reveal the detailed model specification and how to put shocks into the model. One possibility is that the article considers biofuel production in China as a shock – the sectors exist in our model as well, but the production level is not changed as the country does not have a large share of the world biofuel production, and what is more the three crops are self-sufficient in China. Another possibility is that their model assumes farm-land conversion, which affects the impacts of biofuel production on the prices of wheat and rice. Taking into account the facts that in China nearly 80% of ethanol production is from maize (APEC, 2008) and there was relatively little conversion of cultivated land from wheat or rice to maize during the relevant period (although more farm-land was given to maize), the results are difficult to be justified by the assumption (Figure 6.5).

[1] The estimates are calculated as (47.8−32.7)/32.7 and (31.0−24.7)/24.7.

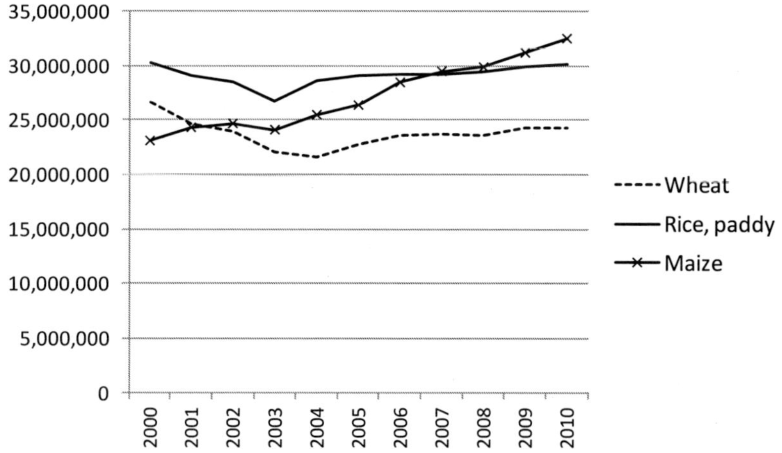

Figure 6.5: Area harvested of grains in China [Unit: hectare]
Data source: FAOSTAT

Policy Discussions

Lifting export restrictions would have stabilised grain prices, especially the rice price, in the global market and LDCs. As the domestic grain price rose through exports even in major exporting countries such as Australia, it might have been reasonable for Russia, a major exporter of grains, to impose export taxes on grains. Furthermore, the export restrictions of major exporting nations like India might have been followed by speculators, who accelerate the price hike. Hence, removing the restrictions would have been beneficial in preventing the grain price hikes. Meanwhile, export restrictions limit farmers' ability to sell their products at higher prices. If it is a large exporting country like Thailand, the damage from restrictions will be much greater than the benefit of curbing domestic price rises. As mentioned in Section 4.1, the number of net sellers of agricultural products is key to the question of whether poverty is increased by the high price of crops. Combining this with our simulation results shows that poverty would have been aggravated if the share of net sellers of rice in the total population had clearly exceeded that of net buyers in the country. In other words, poor countries having many net buyers of grains could have benefited from imposing export restrictions. This is a trade-off between protecting opportunities for farmers to make more profit by selling grains at higher prices and safeguarding consumers by suppressing domestic price increases. Therefore, each country has different optimal export tax rates for grains in order to maximise the welfare of households when there are grain price hikes in the global markets.

Biofuel production raises the maize price in the global market but not in LDCs, and the oil price hike raises the price of crops (except wheat) in LDCs to some extent. These findings mean that manufacturing biofuel from non-food feedstock, as proposed by the G8, would contribute to curbing the international maize price. Even if the oil price does spike, the maize price is less likely to be affected if biofuel is manufactured with non-food material. Nonetheless, net maize-exporting countries like Cambodia (which exported 50% of its production in 2008) would miss opportunities to make greater profits with higher maize prices. Yet, many LDCs would not have seriously suffered from biofuel production in 2008 because of the isolation of their domestic maize markets – contrary to the popular notion that food prices in poor nations were increased by biofuel. While the petroleum price increase makes greater profits for LDCs and their currencies appreciate as some are rich in oil, the general commodity price rise would have reduced the income of workers who are not involved in the oil industries, even considering the spillover effects of greater income as a result of the much increased oil price.

Buffer stocks of grains are versatile in absorbing shocks. If the grain reserve rate is maintained at high level, it will be less likely to trigger food speculation even if demand-supply shocks lead to events such as export bans. Many countries reduced their stock rates to save cost with "just-in-time" management, but the ratio of world stock to usage should be drawn back to the previous level of 26% if speculative activities account for much of the residual of the impacts of our simulations. A negative side of keeping the rate high is the expensive managing cost that includes labour, land rent, depreciation of capital stocks etc. Furthermore, although low-income countries suffer from food price hikes more than rich countries, it is more difficult for poor nations to hold sufficient grain stocks. However, this problem might be overcome by the levels of international grain stocks stated in the 2008 G8 meeting (Maeda and Kano, 2008).

Speculation is not examined in this study, but some papers stress it as a convincing underlying factor (Wei, 2008; Piesse and Thirtle, 2009;, Cooke and Robles, 2009). If much of the unexplainable portion of our simulation is accounted for by speculative activities, regulating them would have weakened the price spikes of grains. Cissokho et al. (2011) propose to impose a transaction tax on all financial investments in food commodities. Yet, we should not overlook the fact that farmers are hedging risks on futures markets. So, whilst the regulations of food speculation protect consumers, the commodity futures markets contribute to risk management of producers.

Conclusion

Through Chapters 4 to 6, we attempt to identify the underlying factors behind the grain price rises in 2008 and analyse the transmitted impacts on LDCs' economies. In Chapter 4, the background is introduced, and the potential factors of the world and LDCs' grain markets are discussed with literature reviews. Chapter 5 conducts a discussion on the models used in earlier studies, and describes the model structure, dataset, and scenarios.

Chapter 6 shows the simulation results of the two types of research, and derives policy implications based on the calculation outcomes. We find that the crop failures, export restrictions and biofuel are the greatest contributory factors among the four for the international price of wheat, rice and maize. Nevertheless, the price increases in 2008 are not fully explained by the four factors, and around 80% of the price hikes is still unexplained. Regarding the prices of wheat and rice, the poor harvest shocks and export restrictions are most critical among the four factors, but biofuel production does not increase the maize price as much as in popular notion. This is because only a little amount of maize is exported and imported, and therefore the international price movement is not transmitted to the LDCs economies to a large degree. The price hikes of wheat and maize in LDCs are not sufficiently accounted for by all the four factors. For example, the analysis of the world price rises finds explanations for about 60% of the rice price increase. However, the robustness analyses demonstrate a certain unreliability of the elasticity of substitution for a value-added composite which implies that the simulated rice price hikes by the export restrictions can be underestimated with the value of 0.2 for agricultural sectors. However, the period of the price spikes is only one or two years, which cannot be long enough for labour forces to move across sectors responding to wage while part of unskilled labour could change industries even for such a short span.

A limitation of the analyses is that the residual of the price hikes could not be anatomised while we evaluated the impacts of the primary real-side factors on food prices. In particular, financial-side factors such as speculation and the US dollar devaluation are left in the remainder if we follow the outcomes from past research although other real-side factors not examined in this analysis might also have affected the grain prices.

Appendix: Sensitivity Analyses

Decomposition analysis of the world grain price hikes

In this section we conduct the robustness tests for the main conclusions of the decomposition analysis by changing elasticity values: the Armington elasticity, the elasticity for value added composite, the elasticity of food composite for household, and the elasticity of substitution between energy goods in both production and household consumption.[2]

Many of the results support our primary conclusions, but the elasticity of substitution among factors greatly influences the decomposition outcome. First, the shares of impact of Scenario A assuming the elasticity between 0.1 and 1.0 have wide ranges (Tables A6.3 and A6.4). If 0.1 is assumed, the impact of Scenario A is 37% while it is only 4% when assuming 1.0. Additionally, if 1.0 is assumed, the effect of biofuel is negative and obviously not the largest among the four. Relatively, rice is less affected by the parameter change. This is because the primal factors for wheat and maize price are poor harvest and biofuel production, respectively, both of which are directly related to the factor substitutability while the largest determinant for rice is export restrictions. Therefore, the results for rice are found to be more robust than those of wheat and maize.

Table A6.1: Decomposition analysis (the Armington elasticity = 20 for agricultural sectors)

Scenario	Change in Price [%]			Share of Impact [%]		
	Wheat	Rice	Maize	Wheat	Rice	Maize
Actual Price Rises	75.0	152.0	67.0	100.0	100.0	100.0
Impact of;						
C (Crop Failure)	5.9	-0.1	-0.1	7.8	-0.1	-0.2
R (Export Restrictions)	3.0	13.3	0.7	4.0	8.7	1.1
P (Petroleum Price Rise)	2.6	0.3	3.0	3.4	0.2	4.5
B (Biofuel Production)	-1.3	-1.4	4.8	-1.8	-0.9	7.2
Interactive Effects	1.9	-0.4	-0.1	2.6	-0.3	-0.1
A (All)	12.0	11.8	8.4	16.0	7.8	12.5
The Rest (Actual Price Rises - A)	63.0	140.2	58.6	84.0	92.2	87.5

[2] The elasticity values are indicated in Table 5.4.

Table A6.2: Decomposition analysis (the Armington elasticity = −50% for agricultural sectors)

Scenario	Change in Price [%]			Share of Impact [%]		
	Wheat	Rice	Maize	Wheat	Rice	Maize
Actual Price Rises	75.0	152.0	67.0	100.0	100.0	100.0
Impact of;						
C (Crop Failure)	8.4	-0.1	-0.2	11.2	-0.1	-0.3
R (Export Restrictions)	4.3	14.5	0.1	5.7	9.6	0.1
P (Petroleum Price Rise)	3.3	-0.1	3.4	4.4	0.0	5.1
B (Biofuel Production)	-1.5	-1.5	8.0	-2.0	-1.0	11.9
Interactive Effects	1.5	-0.6	-0.5	2.0	-0.4	-0.8
A (All)	16.0	12.3	10.7	21.3	8.1	16.0
The Rest (Actual Price Rises - A)	59.0	139.7	56.3	78.7	91.9	84.0

Table A6.3: Decomposition analysis (elasticity of substitution for value added = 0.1)

Scenario	Change in Price [%]			Share of Impact [%]		
	Wheat	Rice	Maize	Wheat	Rice	Maize
Actual Price Rises	75.0	152.0	67.0	100.0	100.0	100.0
Impact of;						
C (Crop Failure)	12.1	-0.2	-0.4	16.2	-0.1	-0.6
R (Export Restrictions)	5.4	19.8	-0.2	7.2	13.0	-0.3
P (Petroleum Price Rise)	3.0	0.5	4.2	4.0	0.3	6.3
B (Biofuel Production)	-1.8	-1.7	22.2	-2.4	-1.1	33.1
Interactive Effects	4.5	-0.7	-0.8	6.0	-0.5	-1.3
A (All)	23.2	17.7	25.0	31.0	11.6	37.3
The Rest (Actual Price Rises - A)	51.8	134.3	42.0	69.0	88.4	62.7

Table A6.4: Decomposition analysis (elasticity of substitution for value added = 1.0)

Scenario	Change in Price [%]			Share of Impact [%]		
	Wheat	Rice	Maize	Wheat	Rice	Maize
Actual Price Rises	75.0	152.0	67.0	100.0	100.0	100.0
Impact of;						
C (Crop Failure)	3.4	0.0	0.0	4.5	0.0	-0.1
R (Export Restrictions)	1.8	8.0	0.4	2.5	5.3	0.6
P (Petroleum Price Rise)	3.1	-0.9	2.7	4.2	-0.6	4.1
B (Biofuel Production)	-1.0	-1.0	-0.6	-1.3	-0.7	-0.9
Interactive Effects	0.3	-0.5	-0.1	0.4	-0.3	-0.2
A (All)	7.7	5.5	2.4	10.3	3.6	3.5
The Rest (Actual Price Rises - A)	67.3	146.5	64.6	89.7	96.4	96.5

Table A6.5: Decomposition analysis (elasticity of substitution for food composite = 1.0)

Scenario	Change in Price [%]			Share of Impact [%]		
	Wheat	Rice	Maize	Wheat	Rice	Maize
Actual Price Rises	75.0	152.0	67.0	100.0	100.0	100.0
Impact of;						
C (Crop Failure)	5.1	0.0	0.0	6.8	0.0	-0.1
R (Export Restrictions)	2.8	8.6	0.4	3.7	5.6	0.6
P (Petroleum Price Rise)	2.9	0.2	3.0	3.8	0.1	4.5
B (Biofuel Production)	-1.3	-1.2	6.3	-1.8	-0.8	9.4
Interactive Effects	0.8	-0.4	-0.3	1.0	-0.3	-0.4
A (All)	10.2	7.2	9.4	13.6	4.7	14.0
The Rest (Actual Price Rises - A)	64.8	144.8	57.6	86.4	95.3	86.0

Table A6.6: Decomposition analysis (elasticity of substitution for energy goods = +45%)

Scenario	Change in Price [%]			Share of Impact [%]		
	Wheat	Rice	Maize	Wheat	Rice	Maize
Actual Price Rises	75.0	152.0	67.0	100.0	100.0	100.0
Impact of;						
C (Crop Failure)	7.2	-0.1	-0.2	9.6	-0.1	-0.3
R (Export Restrictions)	3.6	14.2	0.2	4.9	9.3	0.4
P (Petroleum Price Rise)	2.4	-0.6	2.5	3.1	-0.4	3.8
B (Biofuel Production)	-1.4	-1.5	8.1	-1.9	-1.0	12.1
Interactive Effects	1.1	-0.9	-0.6	1.5	-0.6	-0.9
A (All)	13.0	11.1	10.1	17.3	7.3	15.1
The Rest (Actual Price Rises - A)	62.0	140.9	56.9	82.7	92.7	84.9

Table A6.7: Decomposition analysis (elasticity of substitution for energy goods = −45%)

Scenario	Change in Price [%]			Share of Impact [%]		
	Wheat	Rice	Maize	Wheat	Rice	Maize
Actual Price Rises	75.0	152.0	67.0	100.0	100.0	100.0
Impact of;						
C (Crop Failure)	7.2	-0.1	-0.2	9.6	-0.1	-0.3
R (Export Restrictions)	3.6	14.2	0.2	4.9	9.3	0.4
P (Petroleum Price Rise)	3.9	1.0	4.3	5.2	0.7	6.4
B (Biofuel Production)	-1.4	-1.5	8.1	-1.9	-1.0	12.1
Interactive Effects	1.9	-0.1	0.1	2.5	0.0	0.1
A (All)	15.2	13.6	12.5	20.3	8.9	18.7
The Rest (Actual Price Rises - A)	59.8	138.4	54.5	79.7	91.1	81.3

Decomposition analysis of the price spikes in LDCs

With varying the elasticity of substitution, the robustness of the outcome is checked below. The key findings are that wheat price is pushed up by the poor harvest and export restrictions while it is pulled down by oil price rise; the rice price is explained more than half by Scenario A; and biofuel production does not greatly affect maize price in LDCs.

Crop failure and export restrictions contribute to wheat price. On the other hand, the petroleum price hike reduces it in all the tests. As stated in Section 6.3, the elasticity of substitution among factors is a key parameter that varies the results to a great extent, and less than 50% of the rice price spike is accounted for by all the factors when assuming the elasticity to be 1.0; however, this is not plausible in the study since the period is not long enough for labour mobility. Also, assuming the food composite elasticity for household consumption to be 1.0, the explanatory power of the rice price is lower than 50%. However, the literature review shown in the Appendix of Chapter 3 shows that 1.0 is too large for grains. Biofuel production does not significantly influence the maize price in the original analysis, but if the elasticity of the Armington function is assumed to be 20 for agricultural sectors, the impact is 3%, which is slightly higher than the original decomposition analysis.

Table A6.8: Decomposition analysis (the Armington elasticity = 20 for agricultural sectors)

Scenario	Change in Price [%]			Share of Impact [%]		
	Wheat	Rice	Maize	Wheat	Rice	Maize
Actual Price Rises	66.0	30.0	63.0	100.0	100.0	100.0
Impact of;						
C (Crop Failure)	5.1	-0.1	-0.1	7.7	-0.3	-0.1
R (Export Restrictions)	2.9	9.5	-0.3	4.4	31.7	-0.5
P (Petroleum Price Rise)	-1.5	7.5	2.8	-2.3	24.9	4.4
B (Biofuel Production)	-0.2	-0.3	2.6	-0.3	-1.0	4.1
Interactive Effects	1.8	1.6	-0.1	2.7	5.4	-0.1
A (All)	8.0	18.2	4.9	12.2	60.8	7.7
The Rest (Actual Price Rises - A)	58.0	11.8	58.1	87.8	39.2	92.3

Table A6.9: Decomposition analysis (the Armington elasticity = −50% for agricultural sectors)

Scenario	Change in Price [%]			Share of Impact [%]		
	Wheat	Rice	Maize	Wheat	Rice	Maize
Actual Price Rises	66.0	30.0	63.0	100.0	100.0	100.0
Impact of;						
C (Crop Failure)	6.7	-0.1	-0.1	10.1	-0.4	-0.2
R (Export Restrictions)	7.6	9.9	-1.1	11.5	32.9	-1.8
P (Petroleum Price Rise)	-1.0	7.1	5.8	-1.5	23.8	9.2
B (Biofuel Production)	-0.3	-0.3	0.0	-0.5	-1.1	0.1
Interactive Effects	1.8	2.0	-0.3	2.7	6.6	-0.5
A (All)	14.8	18.5	4.3	22.4	61.7	6.8
The Rest (Actual Price Rises - A)	51.2	11.5	58.7	77.6	38.3	93.2

Table A6.10: Decomposition analysis (elasticity of substitution for value added = 0.1)

Scenario	Change in Price [%]			Share of Impact [%]		
	Wheat	Rice	Maize	Wheat	Rice	Maize
Actual Price Rises	66.0	30.0	63.0	100.0	100.0	100.0
Impact of;						
C (Crop Failure)	10.2	-0.2	-0.3	15.5	-0.7	-0.4
R (Export Restrictions)	6.7	14.4	-2.5	10.1	47.8	-4.0
P (Petroleum Price Rise)	-1.6	9.3	10.7	-2.4	31.0	17.0
B (Biofuel Production)	-0.5	-0.5	1.6	-0.8	-1.6	2.6
Interactive Effects	4.4	3.3	-1.3	6.7	11.0	-2.0
A (All)	19.2	26.3	8.3	29.1	87.5	13.1
The Rest (Actual Price Rises - A)	46.8	3.8	54.7	70.9	12.5	86.9

Table A6.11: Decomposition analysis (elasticity of substitution for value added = 1.0)

Scenario	Change in Price [%]			Share of Impact [%]		
	Wheat	Rice	Maize	Wheat	Rice	Maize
Actual Price Rises	66.0	30.0	63.0	100.0	100.0	100.0
Impact of;						
C (Crop Failure)	2.6	0.0	0.0	4.0	-0.1	0.0
R (Export Restrictions)	3.2	5.5	-0.2	4.8	18.2	-0.3
P (Petroleum Price Rise)	-0.9	4.5	2.0	-1.4	15.1	3.1
B (Biofuel Production)	0.0	-0.1	0.0	0.0	-0.4	0.0
Interactive Effects	0.5	0.6	0.0	0.8	1.9	0.0
A (All)	5.4	10.4	1.8	8.2	34.6	2.8
The Rest (Actual Price Rises - A)	60.6	19.6	61.2	91.8	65.4	97.2

Table A6.12: Decomposition analysis (elasticity of substitution for food composite = 1.0)

Scenario	Change in Price [%]			Share of Impact [%]		
	Wheat	Rice	Maize	Wheat	Rice	Maize
Actual Price Rises	66.0	30.0	63.0	100.0	100.0	100.0
Impact of;						
C (Crop Failure)	4.2	0.0	0.0	6.4	0.0	0.0
R (Export Restrictions)	4.4	4.1	0.2	6.7	13.8	0.2
P (Petroleum Price Rise)	-0.9	5.1	4.7	-1.4	16.9	7.4
B (Biofuel Production)	-0.2	-0.2	0.0	-0.3	-0.5	0.0
Interactive Effects	1.1	0.5	0.1	1.7	1.6	0.1
A (All)	8.6	9.5	4.9	13.0	31.7	7.8
The Rest (Actual Price Rises - A)	57.4	20.5	58.1	87.0	68.3	92.2

Table A6.13: Decomposition analysis (elasticity of substitution for energy goods = +45%)

Scenario	Change in Price [%]			Share of Impact [%]		
	Wheat	Rice	Maize	Wheat	Rice	Maize
Actual Price Rises	66.0	30.0	63.0	100.0	100.0	100.0
Impact of;						
C (Crop Failure)	5.8	-0.1	-0.1	8.8	-0.3	-0.2
R (Export Restrictions)	5.0	9.8	-1.1	7.5	32.7	-1.7
P (Petroleum Price Rise)	-1.3	6.7	5.4	-1.9	22.4	8.5
B (Biofuel Production)	-0.2	-0.3	0.2	-0.3	-1.1	0.4
Interactive Effects	1.2	1.6	-0.3	1.9	5.4	-0.5
A (All)	10.5	17.7	4.1	16.0	59.0	6.6
The Rest (Actual Price Rises - A)	55.5	12.3	58.9	84.0	41.0	93.4

Table A6.14: Decomposition analysis (elasticity of substitution for energy goods = −45%)

Scenario	Change in Price [%]			Share of Impact [%]		
	Wheat	Rice	Maize	Wheat	Rice	Maize
Actual Price Rises	66.0	30.0	63.0	100.0	100.0	100.0
Impact of;						
C (Crop Failure)	5.8	-0.1	-0.1	8.8	-0.3	-0.2
R (Export Restrictions)	5.0	9.8	-1.1	7.5	32.7	-1.7
P (Petroleum Price Rise)	-1.4	8.1	6.4	-2.1	27.1	10.1
B (Biofuel Production)	-0.2	-0.3	0.2	-0.4	-1.1	0.3
Interactive Effects	1.8	2.4	-0.3	2.7	8.1	-0.5
A (All)	10.9	19.9	5.1	16.6	66.4	8.1
The Rest (Actual Price Rises - A)	55.1	10.1	57.9	83.4	33.6	91.9

CHAPTER SEVEN

CONCLUSION

TETSUJI TANAKA

Introduction

The book has evaluated the risk posed to secure food supply by a number of factors, and examined them through three empirical studies. This chapter summarises each chapter. It then describes the methodological contribution of the book and sets out the policy implications which can be derived from the analysis. Finally, the chapter sets out the limitations of the analyses.

Chapter 2 showed the methodology used in the book. In the first part, we outlined the composition of a simple single-country and global SAM with the GTAP database. Next, the equations of a single-country CGE model were represented, and then it was extended to a world scale. In addition, the model was delineated as it was transformed for Chapter 3 including the Monte Carlo method. On the basis of the model for Chapter 3, the model modifications for Chapters 4, 5, and 6 were also explained.

Chapter 3 addressed Japan's rice import liberalisation issue. While free trade is said to enhance the efficiency of resource allocation, the deeper interdependency of food supply is regarded as a threatening factor for the importing side. Most of the literature concluded that lowering trade barriers improves the economic welfare of the importing country with the focus only on the deterministic impacts, but, hence, do not answer how risky the rice trade liberalisation is. Developing a stochastic CGE model, we assessed the risk of the rice trade liberalisation. It was found that trade liberalisation is highly unlikely to endanger Japan's economy by rice productivity shocks in the world. However, household welfare in Japan is considerably hampered by the export bans on rice by the top four rice exporters to Japan. Given that Japan has experienced only a soybean export embargo by the U.S since World War II, the benefit from liberalisation will exceed the damage suffered from it. Further, the emergency rice reserve kept by the government is too large to be cost effective.

In Chapter 4, we introduced the background of the world food crisis in 2008 to clarify the objectives of the two studies: the identification of the driving forces behind the 2008 world grain price rises; and establishing the factors in the local grain markets in LDCs. The background includes the food price increases in the international market, food riots in poor countries, the responses of governments, existing literature concerning price transmission between world and local markets in developing countries, and the influences of high agricultural prices on poverty. Then, nine primal potential factors behind the grain price rises were outlined. These were: the demand growth in China and India, decline of grain productivity, extreme weather pattern, oil price hike, emergence of biofuel, export restrictions, devaluation of the US dollar, food speculation and the low level of world grain stocks. These were discussed with data and reference to past literature. Finally, the studies which estimate the effects of a factor(s) on developing economies were reviewed.

Chapter 5 showed the methodology applied to the two analyses. Firstly, we critically reviewed the models that quantify the impacts of the possible price drivers. Secondly, the model structure was briefly described. Next, the regional and sectoral aggregations, the method of creating new sectors (maize, bioethanol, and biodiesel sectors) in the original GTAP database, elasticity parameters, and price data were outlined. Finally, the scenario factors were outlined, namely crop failure, export restrictions, oil price hike, and biofuel production, and the scenarios were indicated.

Chapter 6 demonstrated the simulation results of the two analyses, and discussed policy implications. The principal findings for the drivers of the world grain price hikes were that the four real-side factors poorly explain the global price rises while crop failure, export restrictions and biofuel production are crucial factors for the prices of wheat, rice, and maize, respectively. The same four shocks also account little for the LDCs' price hikes of wheat and maize but over 50% of the rice price spike is explained by the factors, especially by export restrictions. Another interesting outcome is that biofuel productions do not raise the maize price in LDCs as the regions have neither much export nor import of maize. Based on the results, we derive policy implications related to export restrictions, biofuel policy, buffer grain stocks and the regulation of speculative activities.

Methodological contribution

The methodological contribution of the book is the application of the Monte Carlo method to a CGE model. On the topic of Chapter 3, the literature inspects the liberalisation policy, measuring only the deterministic effects of Japan lowering trade barriers on rice, and cannot touch the core question of securing its food supply after the free trade. However, the application of the method to a CGE model makes it possible to evaluate the stochastic impacts of productivity shocks on the economy from liberalisation, and to clarify the true benefits (or losses) from abolishing the import tariff on rice. In the study of Chapter 3, the distribution of rice productivity shocks is assumed to follow the independent identically distributed normal distribution, but as long as the form of distribution is specified, it is possible to assess the probabilistic effects of other types of variable shocks.

Policy implications

Trade liberalisation

The closed rice market in Japan does not necessarily enhance the security of food supply according to our simulations. Firstly, the effects of productivity shocks from abroad are not significant, and productivity shocks in Japan are considerably more influential on Japan's households than those from the outside of Japan. Therefore, free trade raises the mean of welfare of Japan, and what is more, the variance of welfare is smaller than without liberalisation. Although our simulations show that rice export bans by major four trade partners for Japan certainly reduce household welfare in Japan, it still exceeds 2000 kcal/day/person, which is defined as the most serious level by the MAFF. Moreover, our simulation outcomes suggest that if rice export is banned by the major exporting countries every three or four years, the trade should not be liberalised, in terms of the economic damage. However, from a historical viewpoint, Japan has experienced only one export embargo from the US on soybean since after the World War II.

The participation in the Trans-Pacific Partnership (TPP) agreement has aroused a fierce debate in Japan, which involves agricultural sectors. The major objections are concerned with stable food supply and unemployment. The former is the subject examined in Chapter 3. Also many of Japan's nationals focus on the self-sufficiency rate of food as a means to guarantee their food supply, but we demonstrate that self-sufficiency does not necessarily enhance Japan's food security. Farmers in Japan are not competitive against those in the US and Australia who are potential competitors in the agreement because the size of farm-land per farmer in the US and Australia is as 49 and 316 times large as that in Japan in 2008. The government promotes the incorporation of small-scale farmers to increase the number of large-scale ones for greater competitiveness. Taking into account that consumption depends not only on price but also quality, Japan's rice farmers have an advantage as observed in the experience of liberalising the Japan's beef market in 1991. It should not be disregarded but is difficult to assess the environmental value of the rice farming although we do not analyse it in the book.

Grain reserves

The effectiveness of the rice buffer stocks stored by Japan's government is measured in Chapter 3. It is shown that the buffer stocks alleviate negative productivity shocks and contribute to rice price stabilisation. However, the effects of the reserves on welfare do not surpass the annual maintenance cost. Therefore, we conclude that the government keeps too much rice in terms of the cost-effectiveness. The storage cost could be saved by changing to other less expensive locations like Thailand, and then it could hold more rice reserves.

Considering that the grain price impacts of shocks tend to be large when the grain stock level is low, we have shown the sensitivity tests in Chapter 6. However, these do not indicate large differences in the decomposition analyses from the original results – contrary to the inference of existing papers such as Timmer (2008) and Piesse and Thirtle (2009). Grain stocks also have another role, to discourage non-commercial traders from speculating on rising prices. Although our simulations do not focus on speculation as a factor of the 2008 food price inflation, there is a possibility that the combination of the decreased grain reserves with several other shocks such as the poor harvest in Australia might have triggered speculative behaviour as Heady and Fan (2008) argue. In other words, food prices might not have gone up so much if there had been sufficient amount of grain stocks. According to the results of our robustness tests, grain stocks do not significantly influence grain prices, but because we have not examined the amplified effects between speculation, grain reserve and other factors, the impacts of low grain stock level could be underestimated.

During the food crisis, food riots happened only in poor nations. This implies that low-income countries suffered from the price spikes of grains more than rich countries. Yet, national governments lowered their food stock level to save the maintenance costs, which means that destitute countries had greater difficulty in holding sufficient grain stocks. Maeda and Kano (2008) analyse the effectiveness of international rice stock, but this issue should be investigated more in future research.

Export restriction

The analyses of Chapters 4, 5, and 6 demonstrate that export restrictions bring some impacts on food prices in both the world markets and LDCs. This conversely means that the annulment of the restrictions would have lessened the upward volatility but only to a limited degree. However, the rice price in the global and LDCs' markets are affected by export restrictions because international rice market is thinner than other crops, and even major rice exporting countries such as India banned their rice export, which corroborates Heady and Fan (2008).

However, as presented in Chapter 3, the larger the exporter a country is, the greater the sacrifice it needs with its export restrictions. In addition, if the number of net sellers of a crop is greater than that of net buyers, poverty will be raised in the country even if it is not a large exporting country. So, the balance between securing opportunities for farmers to sell their agricultural products at higher prices and keeping down domestic prices for consumers is a dilemma for policy makers when facing international price hikes.

Biofuel policy and energy price

Our simulation results show that the emergence of biofuel raises the price of maize in the world market by only 8% but marginally affects maize prices in LDCs and wheat and rice prices in both the markets. Namely, even if the subsidy for biofuel production was abolished, the price increases in wheat and rice would not have been greatly reduced in 2008. A proposal by the G8 to manufacture biofuel from non-food feedstock is effective for curbing price rises to a certain extent but only for the international maize price.

The oil price hike in 2008 increased the grain prices moderately in global and LDC markets. Causes of the oil price rise are not our focus, but if it had been raised mainly by speculation, the Oil Trading Transparency Act discussed in the United States Senate to strengthen the regulation on oil speculation will work for weakening the oil price fluctuations, but will have a limited impact on grain prices. Since the oil price hike stimulates biofuel demand as a substitute, manufacturing biofuel from non-food materials will further diminish the impact of an oil price increase on food prices.

Meanwhile, the suppression of maize price rises implies that maize producers may fail to exploit the advantage of selling their maize at more expensive prices. Some LDCs are net exporters of maize, but as indicated in our studies, since the maize market in LDCs is rather isolated from other regions, the price is not seriously affected.

LDCs include several oil-producing countries. The oil price spike appreciates the LDCs' currencies, which makes the domestic wheat price cheaper because around 30% of wheat consumption is dependent on imports while the prices of rice and maize increase as a consequence of not having much international trade in the products. Nevertheless, workers from outside the oil industry in LDCs would not have been blessed with the petroleum price increase, but rather will have seen their real income cut by commodity inflation.

The US Congress allowed a subsidy for ethanol production to expire at the end of 2011 (Lever, 2012). In addition to that, bioethanol produced from maize is not very competitive to oil without a subsidy (Kawashima, 2009). These facts suggest that bioethanol production in the US will be substantially discouraged from 2012.

Regulation of speculation

Although we do not analyse the effects of speculation in this book, some papers regard it as a principal factor for the food price hikes in 2008 (Cooke and Robles, 2009;, Wei, 2008; Piesse and Thirtle, 2009). If this is true, restraining speculation on food markets will be effective in reducing the price volatility while the futures market functions as a means of risk-hedging for farmers.

As a matter of fact, the EU tries to levy a tax called "Tobin tax" on financial transactions to dis-incentivise short-term capital flows (Pop, 2012). Yet, a major problem is that if there is a region that will not agree with and will not introduce the tax, it can be a loophole for speculation. Especially regions that have attracted financial institutions by favourable tax rates so-called offshore tax havens will not be likely to ratify the agreement. Although it is difficult to impose the financial transaction tax over the whole world, over 600 agreements on tax transparency and information exchange have been made since April 2009 (G20-G8 France 2011, 2011).

The Bank of Thailand legislated regulations on the foreign exchange market in 2006 to control short-term capital flows by requiring investors to deposit 30% of the investment money into the Bank of Thailand, which was returned to them if the funds have remained within the country for one year (Tongurai, 2008). In 1991, Chile put capital controls into effect, which were found to be significantly effective on capital inflows (Gregorio et al., 2000).Thus, even if speculation had been an influential factor in the 2008 food crisis, there are still some obstacles to overcome in enforcing the restrictions, and the issue should be studied.

Limitations of research

The reservations of the studies of this book need to be acknowledged. First, political aspects are not considered in the analyses. Chapter 3 discusses the rice trade liberalisation by Japan's government, which is a politically sensitive issue since the rice farmers in Japan hold an influential number of votes, and the government, more specifically the MAFF, has persistently agitated to protect domestic farming. The chapter has demonstrated the potential benefit (or risk) from liberalising the rice imports, but it does not suggest the possibility of the implementation of the policy. For the implementation of the policy, the political system needs to be discussed with the result of Chapter 3.

Secondly, the trustworthiness of CGE outputs has to be examined. Kehoe et al. (1995), for instance, confirm that a CGE model perform well in forecasting the changes in relative prices and resource allocation in the 1986 Spanish fiscal reform, comparing with historical record. Thus, some other articles affirm the usefulness of CGE models to some extent under some conditions in the area of free trade, energy, agricultural commodity prices and so on (Hertel et al., 2007; Beckman and Hertel, 2010; Valenzuela et al., 2007.). Conversely, Kehoe (2003) argues that a few most prominent static general equilibrium models extremely underestimate the effects of the North American Free Trade Agreement (NAFTA), and Hertel et al. (2004) also point out that the GTAP-AGR model holds the incapability of reproducing wheat market price volatility. In this book, the robustness of the primary conclusions has been fully checked with sensitivity analyses but publications concerning this subject are very rare, especially given the recent increase in CGE model usage.

BIBLIOGRAPHY

Abbott, P. C., Christopher, H., and Wallace, E. T., 2009. What's Driving Food Prices?: March 2009 update. Farm Foundation Issue Report.

Abbott, P. C., Christopher, H., and Wallace, E. T., 2008. What's Driving Food Prices? Farm Foundation Issue Report.

Aksoy, M. A., and Isik-Dikmelik, A., 2008. Are Low Food Prices Pro-Poor?: Net Food Buyers and Sellers in Low-Income Countries. Policy Research Working Paper 4642, The World Bank.

Aloisi, S., 2011. France, FAO see food crisis risk as prices soar. 4 February 2011, Reuters. http://uk.reuters.com/article/2011/02/04/uk-food-crisis-idUKTRE7132NZ20110204

Anderson, K., Martin, W., van der Mensbrugghe, D., 2006. Market and welfare implications of Doha reform scenarios, in: Anderson, K., Martin, W. (Eds.), Agricultural Trade Reform and the Doha Development Agenda. The World Bank, Washington, DC, pp. 333–399.

Asian-Pacific Economic Cooperation (APEC), 2008. China biofuels activities. http://www.biofuels.apec.org/me_china.html.

Armington, P. S., 1969. A theory of demand for products distinguished by place of production. International Monetary Fund Staff Pap. 16(1), 159–178.

Arndt, C., Benfica, R., Maximiano, N., Nucifora, A. M. D., and Thurlow, T., 2008. Higher Fuel and Food Prices: Impacts and Responses for Mozambique. Agricultural Economics 39, 497-511.

Baffes, J., 1997. Explaining stationary variable with non-stationary regressors. Applied Economic Letters (4), 69-75.

Barrett, C. B., and Dorosh, P. A., 1996. Farmers' Welfare and Changing Food Prices: Nonparametric Evidence from Rice in Madagascar. American Journal of Agricultural Economics 78, 656-669.

Bchir, M., Decreux, H. Y., Guérin, J. and Jean, S., 2002. MIRAGE, A computable general equilibrium model for trade policy analysis, December CEPII working paper, No 2002–17.

Beckman, J., Hertel, T. W., and Tyner, W., 2011. Validating Energy-oriented CGE Models. Energy Economics Article in press.

Burniaux, J., and Truong, T. P., 2002. GTAP-E: An energy-environmental version of the GTAP model. GTAP Technical Paper No. 16.

Charlebois, P., 2008. The Impact on World Price of Cereals and Oilseeds of Export Restriction Policies. Agriculture and Agri-Food Canada, Ottawa, Ontario.

Chern, W. S., 2001. Assessment of demand-side factors affecting global food security. in: Chern, W. S., Carter, C. A., Shei, S. (Eds.), Food Security in Asia. Edward Elgar, Cheltenham, pp. 83–118.

Chern, W. S., Ishibashi, K., Taniguchi, K., Tokoyama Y., 2002. Analysis of food Consumption behavior by Japanese households. ESA Working Paper No. 02-06, The Food and Agriculture Organization.

Chino, J., 2000. Kome jukyu moderu-no kozo-to seisan-chosei-no yukue [Demand-supply model and perspectives of set-aside policy in Japanese rice economy]. in: Morishima, N. (Ed.), Kokkyo-sochi-to Nihn-nogyo [Trade Policy and Japanese Agriculture]. Norin-tokei-kyokai, Tokyo, pp. 234–252 (in Japanese).

Cissokho, M., Lines, T., Nissanke, M., and Smith, A., 2011. Food security, finance and international trade; how to protect developing countries from volatile global markets. Veblen Institute for Economic Reforms, September.

Cooke, B., and R. Robles, 2009. Recent Food Prices Movements: A Time Series Analysis. IFPRI Discussion Paper No. 00942, International Food Policy Research Institute, Washington, DC.

Cramer, G. L., Hansen, J. M., Wailes, E. J., 1999. Impact of rice tariffication on Japan and the world rice market. Am. J. Agric. Econ. 81(5), 1149–1156.

Cramer, G. L., Wailes, E. J., Shui, S., 1993. Impacts of liberalizing trade in the world rice market. Am. J. Agric. Econ. 75(1), 219–226.

Christiaensen, L., and Demery, L., 2007. Down to earth: agriculture and poverty reduction in Africa. The World Bank.

Cudjoe, G., Breisinger, C., and Diao, X., 2010. Local Impacts of a Global Crisis: Food Price Transmission, Consumer Welfare, and Poverty in Ghana. Food Policy 35, 294-302.

Dervis, K., Melo, J. de, and Robinson, S., 1982. General Equilibrium Models for Development Policy, Cambridge University Press.

Devarajan, S., Lewis, J. D., Robinson, S., 1990. Policy lessons from trade-focused, two-sector models. J. Policy Modeling 12(4), 625–657.

Dessus, S, Herrera, S., and Hoyos de R, 2008. The impact of food inflation on urban poverty and its monetary cost: some back-of-the-envelope calculations. World Bank Policy Research Working Paper 4666.

Francois, J. F. and Roland-Holst, D. W., 1997. Scale economies and imperfect Competition. in Francois, J. F. and Reinert, K. A. (eds.) Applied methods for trade policy analysis: a handbook, New York: Cambridge University Press, Chap. 11, pp. 331–363.

F.O. Licht, 2010. World ethanol and biofuels report. Vol. 9 (08).

G8 Information Centre, 2008. G8 Summits, Hokkaido Official Documents, G8 Leaders Statements on Global Food Security.

G20-G8 France 2011, 2011. Address by the president of the French Republic, Press conference to present the presidency of the G20 and G8. Monday, 24 January 2011. http://www.g20-g8.com/g8-g20/g8/english/for-the-press/news-releases/press-conference-by-nicolas-sarkozy-monday-24.933.html.

Gilbert, C., 1989. The impact of exchange rate changes and developing country debt on commodity prices. Economic Journal (99), 773-784.

Gregorio, J. D., Edwards, S., and Valdes, R. O., 2000. Controls on capital inflows: do they work? Journal of Development Economics Vol. 63, 59–83.

Harberger, A. C., 1962. The Incidence of the Corporation Tax. Journal of Political Economy 70, 215-240.

Harris, R. L., Robinson, S., 2001. Economy-wide effects of El Niño/Southern Oscillation (ENSO) in Mexico and the role of improved forecasting and technological change. TMD Discussion Paper No. 83, International Food Policy Research Institute, Washington, DC.

Hasebe, T., 1996. Kome-no hinshitsu-betsu-juyo-to kakaku-hendo [Rice demand by quality and price fluctuation]. in: Kuroyanagi, T., Kada, R. (Eds.), Kome-jiyuka-no keiryo-bunseki [Quantitative Analysis on the Rice Liberalization in Japan]. Taimeido, Tokyo, pp. 13–30 (in Japanese).

Hayami, Y., 2000. Food security: fallacy or reality? in: Chern, S. W., Carter, C. A., Shei, S. (Eds.), Food Security in Asia. Edward Elgar, Cheltenham, pp. 11–17.

Heady, D., and Fan, S., 2008. Anatomy of a crisis: the causes and consequences of surging food prices. IFPRI Discussion Paper 00831.

Hertel, T. W., Hummels, D., Ivanic, M., and Keeney, R., 2007. How Confident Can We Be of CGE-based Assessments of Free Trade Agreements? Economic Modelling vol. 24, issue 4, pages 611-635.

Hertel, T. W., Keeney, R., and Valenzuela, 2004. Global analysis of agricultural trade liberalization: assessing model validity. Selected paper prepared for presentation at the American Agricultural Economics Association Annual Meeting, Denver, Colorado, July 1-4, 2004.

Hertel, T. W. (Ed.), 1997. Global Trade Analysis. Cambridge University Press, Cambridge.

Hosoe, N., 2004. Crop failure, price regulation, and emergency imports of Japan's rice sector in 1993. Appl. Econ. 36(10), 1051–1056.

Hosoe, N., Gasawa, K., and Hashimoto, H., 2010. Textbook of Computable General Equilibrium Modeling: Programming and Simulations. Palgrave Macmillan.

IMF (International Monetary Fund), 2009. IMF Primary Commodity Prices. Website, http://www.imf.org/external/np/res/commod/index.asp.

International Crop Reserve Research Workshop, 2001. Dai-nikai Kokusai Bichiku-koso Kenkyukai-iin Yokyu Shiryo [Materials for the Second Meeting of the International Crop Reserve Research Workshop]. Food Agency, Ministry of Agriculture, Forestry, and Fishery, Government of Japan, Tokyo, June 5 (in Japanese).

IRRI, 2008. The rice crisis: what needs to be done? IRRI's 9-point action plan http://beta.irri.org/solutions/images/irri/the_rice_crisis_summary.pdf.

Ivanic, M., and Martin, W., 2008. Implications of higher global food prices for poverty in low-income countries. Agricultural Economics 39, 405-416.

Jayne, T. S., Yamano, T., Nyoro, J., and Awuor, T., 2001. Do Famers Really Benefit from High Food Prices?: Balancing Rural Interests in Kenya's Maize Pricing and Marketing Policy. Tegemeo Working Paper 2B, Egerton University.

Johansen, L., 1960. Multi-sectoral study of growth. Amsterdam, North-Holland.

Kako, T., Gemma, M., Ito, S., 1997. Implications of the minimum access rice import on supply and demand balance of rice in Japan. Agric. Econ. 16(3): 193–204.

Kawashima, H., 2009. Do not agitate food crisis [shokuryokiki wo aotte ha ikenai]. Bungei Shunju.

Kehoe, T. J., Polo, C., and Sancho, F., 1995. An evaluation of the performance of an applied general equilibrium model of the Spanish economy. Economic Theory vol. 6, pp. 115-141.

Kobayashi, H., 1988. Nihon-no kome-jukyu [Demand and supply of rice in Japan]. in: Oga, K. (Ed.), Kome-no Kokusai-jukyu-to yunyu-jiyuka-mondai [International Trade of Rice and its Trade Liberalization]. Norin-tokei-kyokai, Tokyo, pp. 31–73 (in Japanese).

Krugman, P., 1980. Scale economies, product differentiation, and the pattern of trade. American Economic Review, American Economic Association, vol. 70(5), pages 950-59.

Kusakari, H., 1991. Kome-no hinshitsu-betsu-juyo-to yunyu-jiyuka [Demand for rice by quality and trade liberalization]. in: Kome-seisaku-kenkyukai (Ed.), Kome-yunyu-jiyuka-no eikyo-bunseki [Impacts of Rice Import Liberalization]. Fumin-kyokai, Tokyo, pp.

146–174 (in Japanese).

Lever, R., 2012. US looks ahead after ethanol subsidy expires. 14 January 2012, AFP, http://www.google.com/hostednews/afp/article/ALeqM5jAkrI-Apr7LvZ7QPUQz39oe5Jr4w?docId=CNG.2413163943498a313d9d0bab9035d953.3e1.

Madon, C., 2010. Wheat and corn stockpiles falls as Russian droughts worsens. 12, August, 2010, Daily Finance. http://www.bloggingstocks.com/2010/08/12/wheat-and-corn-stockpiles-fall-as-russian-drought-worsens/

Maeda, K., Kano, H., 2008. Kokusai-kome-bichiku-ni-yoru shokuryo-anzen-hosho-to shijo-anteika—kukan-kinko-moderu-ni-yoru keiryo-bunseki [Food security and market stabilization through international rice reserve stock: A spatial equilibrium analysis]. Nogyo-keizai-kenkyu 79 (4) [J. Rural Econ.], 199–216 (in Japanese).

MAFF (Ministry of Agriculture, Forestry, and Fisheries), 2008. Report on foreign food demand and supply in 2008. (in Japanese) [kaigai shokuryo jukyu repoto 2008].

MAFF (Ministry of Agriculture, Forestry, and Fisheries), Japan, 2006. Fusokuji-no Shokuryo-anzen-hosho Manyuaru [Food Security Manual for Contingency Situations]. Tokyo, April (in Japanese).

MAFF (Ministry of Agriculture, Forestry, and Fisheries), Japan, 2001. Dai-nikai Shokuryo Anzen-hosho Manyuaru Sho-iinkai Giji-roku [Minutes of the Second Meeting of the Subcommittee for the Food Security Manual]. Tokyo, September 26, (in Japanese).

Martin, W. and Winters, L. A. (eds.), 1996. The Uruguay Round and the Developing Countries. New York: Cambridge University Press.

McDonald, S., and Thierfelder, K., 2004. Deriving a global social accounting matrix from GTAP versions 5 and 6 data. GTAP Technical Paper No. 22.

Mensbrugghe, D. van der, 2005. LINKAGE technical reference document version 6. http://siteresources.worldbank.org/INTPROSPECTS/Resources/334934-1100792545130/LinkageTechNote.pdf

Metropolis, N., and Ulam, S. M., 1949. The Monte Carlo method. Journal of the American Statistical Association Vol. 44, No. 247.

Meyers, W. H., and Meyer, S., 2008. Causes & implications of the food price surge. FAPRI-MU Report #12-08, December.

Mitchell, D., 2008. A Note on Rising Food Prices. Policy Research Working Paper 4682, the World Bank, Washington, DC.

Mitra-Kahn, B. H., 2008. Debunking the Myths of Computable General

Equilibrium Models. SCEPA Working Paper 2008-1.

Miyatake, O., and Nakayama, T., 1960. The Monte Carlo method. (in Japanese) Nikkan Kogyo Shinbunsha.

Murphy, S., 2008. The Global Food Crisis: Creating an Opportunity for Fairer and More Sustainable Food and Agriculture System Worldwide. Ecofair Trade Dialogue Discussion Papers No. 11.

Naylor, R., and Falcon, W., 2010. Food security in an era of economic volatility. Population and Development Review Vol. 36 (4), pp. 693-723.

Nganou, J. P., Parra, J. C, and Wodon, Q, 2009. Oil price shocks, poverty, and gender: a social accounting matrix analysis for Kenya. Munich Personal RePEc Archive (MPRA) Paper No. 28471.

Otsuka, K., 1984. Kome-no juyo-kyokyu-kansu-no suitei [Estimation of rice demand and supply functions]. Keizai-to keizaigaku 55 [J. the Faculty of Economics, Tokyo Metropolitan University]: 15–26 (in Japanese).

Parikh, A., 1979. Forecasts of input-output tables using the RAS method. Review of Economics and Statistics, 61 (3), pp. 477-481.

Parra, J. C., and Wodon, Q, 2008. Comparing the impact of food and energy price shocks on consumers: a social accounting matrix analysis for Ghana. World Bank Policy Research Working Paper 4741.

Piesse, J., Thirtle, C., 2009. Three bubbles and a panic: An explanatory review of recent food commodity price events. Food Policy 34 119–129.

Pop, V., 2012. Monti and Merkel: financial tax must cover whole EU. 12 January 2012 euobserver.com, http://euobserver.com/19/114847.

Ravallion, M. and Lokshin, M., 2004. Gainers and losers from trade reform in Morocco. Middle East and North Africa Working Paper Series No. 37, The World Bank.

Reuters, 2008. The movement of export restrictions of rice and buffer stock [kome no yushutsu kisei to zaiko hojuu no ugoki] (in Japanese). http://jp.reuters.com/article/worldNews/idJPJAPAN-31611520080501?pageNumber=4&virtualBrandChannel=0, 1st of May, 2008.

Rice Stable Supply Support Organization, Japan, 2007. Seifu-bichiku-mai-no hanbai-kakaku-no-suii [Sales prices of government rice stocks for emergencies (October of 2007)], December 25 (in Japanese). (http://www.komenet.jp/komedata/kakaku/documents/2007/10/4-10_071225.xls, accessed on September 15, 2010.)

Rosegrant M. W., 2008. Biofuels and Grain Prices: Impacts and Policy Responses. International Food Policy Research Institute, Washington,

DC, May 7.

Rosegrant M. W., Ringler C., Msangi S., Sulser T. B., Zhu T., and Cline S. A., 2008. International model for policy analysis of agricultural commodities and trade (IMPACT): model description. International Food Policy Research Institute website http://www.ifpri.org/book-751/ourwork/program/impact-model.

Rowley, E., 2011. G20 Paris: Nicolas Sarkozy calls for action against inflation's 'great threat'. The Telegraph, 19, February, 2011. http://www.telegraph.co.uk/finance/g20-summit/8334770/G20-Paris-Nicolas-Sarkozy-calls-for-action-against-inflations-great-threat.html

Sawada, M., 1985. Shokuryo-juyo-to hinshitsu [Food demand and quality]. in: Sakiura, S. (Ed.), Keizai-hatten-to nogyo-kaihatsu [Economic Development and Agricultural Development]. Norin-tokei-kyokai, Tokyo, pp. 70–89 (in Japanese).

Sawada, Y., 1984. Komerui-juyo-no keiryo-bunseki [Quantitative analysis of rice demand]. in: Sakiura, S. (Ed.), Kome-no keizai-bunseki [Economic Analysis of Rice]. Norin-tokei-kyokai, Tokyo, pp. 139–153 (in Japanese).

Scarf, H. E., 1973. The Computation of Economic Equilibria, Yale University Press.

Science Council of Japan, 2001. Chikyu-kankyo Ningen-seikatsu-ni-kakawaru Nogyo-oyobi-shinrin-no Tamenteki-na-kino-no Hyoka-ni-tsuite (Toshin) [Report on the Multi-functionality of Agriculture and Forest for Global Environment and Human Life], Tokyo, November (in Japanese).

Sharma, R., 2011. Food Export Restrictions: Review of the 2007-2010 Experience and Considerations for Disciplining Restrictive Measures. FAO Commodity And Trade Policy Research Working Paper No. 32.

Shoven, J. B., and Whalley, J., 1992. Applying General Equilibrium, Cambridge University Press.

Smil, V., 2000. Feeding the World. Massachusetts Institute of Technology.

Taheripour, F., Birur, D. K., Hertel, T. W., and Tyner, W. E., 2008. Introducing Liquid Biofuels into GTAP Data Base. GTAP Research Memorandum No. 11.

Tanaka, T., and Hosoe, N., 2011a. What Drove the Crop Price Hikes in the Food Crisis? GRIPS Discussion Papers 11-16.

Tanaka, T., and Hosoe, N., 2011b. Does Agricultural Trade Liberalization Increase Risks of Supply-side Uncertainty?: Effects of Productivity Shocks and Export Restrictions on Welfare and Food Supply in Japan. Food Policy 36(3), 368–377.

Tongrai, J., 2008. Baht appreciation and the Bank of Thailand's foreign exchange intervention: experience in 2001-March 2008.

Trostle, R., 2008. Global Agricultural Supply and Demand: Factors Contributing to the Recent Increase in Food Commodity Prices. USDA, A Report from the Economic Research Service WRS-0801.

USDA (United States Department of Agriculture), 2008. China, Peoples Republic of, Agricultural Situation, 2008 China Tightens Control on Grain and Flour Exports. GAIN Report No. CH8001, January 14.

Valenzuela, E. and Hertel, T. W., 2007. Assessing Global Computable General Equilibrium Model Validity Using Agricultural Price Volatility. American Journal of Agricultural Economics, vol. 89, issue 2, pages 383-397

Von Braun, J., 2008. Rising Food Prices: What Should Be Done? IFPRI Policy Brief April 2008.

Von Braun, J., Ahmed, A., Asenso-Okyere, K., Fan, S., Gulati, A., Hoddinott, J., Pandya-Lorch, R., Rosegrant, M. W., Ruel, M, Torero, M., Van Rheenen, T., and Von Grebmer, K., 2008. High Food Prices: The What, Who, and How of Proposed Policy Actions. Policy Brief May 2008. IFPRI.

Wailes, E. J., 2005. Rice: global trade, protectionist policies, and the impact of trade liberalization, in: Aksoy, M. A., Beghin, J. C. (Eds.), Global Agricultural Trade and Developing Countries. The World Bank, Washington, DC, pp. 177–193.

Wei Ruan, 2008. World grain price hikes. (in Japanese) [Sekai teki na kokumotsu kakaku no koutou], Nihon Keizai Shinbun, 23, July, 2008.

Whalley, J., 1982. An Evaluation of the Recent Tokyo Round Trade Agreement Using General Equilibrium Computation Methods, Journal of Policy Modelling 4, 341-361.

Wodon, Q., and Zaman, H., 2008. Rising food prices in sub-saharan Africa: poverty impact and Policy responses. World Bank Policy Research Working Paper 4738.

Wodon, Q., Tsimpo, C., Backiny-Yetna, P., Joseph, G., Adoho, F., and Coulombe, H., 2008. Potential impact of higher food prices on poverty: summary estimates for a dozen west and central African countries. World Bank Policy Research Working Paper, 4745.

World Bank, 2011. Food Price Hike Drives 44 Million People into Poverty. No: 2011/333/PREM.

—. 2008a. Competitive Agriculture or State Control: Ukraine's Response to the Global Food Crisis. Europe and Central Asia Region, Sustainable Development Unit, May, Washington DC.

—, 2008b. Group of Eight, Meeting of Finance of Ministers, Osaka,

Addressing the Food Crisis: The Need for Rapid and Coordinated Action.
Wright, B. D., 2011. The Economics of Price Volatility. Applied Economic Perspectives and Policy 33 (1), 32–58.
Yang, J., Qiu, H., Huang, J., and Rozelle, S., 2008. Fighting Global Food Price Rises in the Developing World: The Response of China and its Effect on Domestic and World Markets. Agricultural Economics 39 (1), 453–464.